KF 361. B67 1983

W9-CMO-540

Early American Law
and Society

Early American Law and Society

Stephen Botein
Michigan State University

Generously Donated to
The Frederick Douglass Institute
By Professor Jesse Moore
Fall 2000

ALFRED A. KNOPF   NEW YORK

This book was originally developed as part of an American Bar Association program on law and humanities with major funding from the National Endowment for the Humanities and additional support from the Exxon Education Foundation and Pew Memorial Trust. The ABA established this program to help foster improved understanding among undergraduates of the role of law in society through the creation of a series of volumes in law and humanities. The ABA selected a special advisory committee of scholars, lawyers, and jurists (Commission on Undergraduate Education in Law and the Humanities) to identify appropriate topics and select writers. This book is a revised version of the volume first published by the ABA. However, the writer, and not the American Bar Association, individual members and committees of the Commission, the National Endowment for the Humanities, Exxon Education Foundation, or Pew Memorial Trust, bears sole responsibility for the content, analysis, and conclusion contained herein.

THIS IS A BORZOI BOOK
PUBLISHED BY ALFRED A. KNOPF, INC.

First Edition
9 8 7 6 5 4 3 2 1
Copyright © 1983 by Alfred A. Knopf, Inc.

All rights reserved under International and Pan-American Copyright Conventions. No part of this book may be reproduced in any form or by any means, electronic or mechanical, including photocopying, without permission in writing from the publisher. All inquiries should be addressed to Alfred A. Knopf, Inc., 201 East 50th Street, New York, N.Y. 10022. Published in the United States by Alfred A. Knopf, Inc., New York, and simultaneously in Canada by Random House of Canada Limited, Toronto. Distributed by Random House, Inc., New York.

LIBRARY OF CONGRESS CATALOGING IN PUBLICATION DATA

Botein, Stephen.
    Early American law and society.

    (Borzoi books in law and American society)
    Bibliography: p.
    Includes index.
    1. Law—United States—History and criticism.
2. Sociological jurisprudence.   I. Title.
II. Series.
KF361.B67   1982   349.73   82-17158
ISBN 0-394-33252-0   347.3

Manufactured in the United States of America

Preface

This book is an introduction to the history of early American law, from the first colonizing ventures at the end of the sixteenth century to Independence in 1776. Throughout, for the sake of nonspecialized readers, I have tried to avoid technical legal language. As I hope will be clear from my interpretive essay, the historical study of law is inseparable from the historical study of such subjects as race, religion, family life, and war. Wherever pertinent, then, I have tried to incorporate recent findings by scholars who would not identify themselves as legal historians. Since an introduction to early American law may well serve as an introduction to early American society, the bibliography at the conclusion of this book is not restricted to titles in the sub-field of legal history.

By way of supplementing each of the chapters in my interpretive essay, I have reproduced examples of source material from the period. With the help of headnotes, these are meant to encourage further consideration of broad issues and to indicate some of the complexities involved in reading the legal record of colonial America. I have selected documents with an eye toward representing not only the geographical range of early American history but also the varieties of legal experience in a premodern social environment. Along with formal statements of high theory, some of which may appear to have a certain continuing relevance, there are frequent glimpses of seventeenth- and eighteenth-century controversy in all its grubby and bitter particularity. Teachers wishing to adapt this material for the assignment of written work will recognize that different combinations of documents make it possible to emphasize different themes.

Since beginning this project some three years ago, I have benefited from the support and criticism of more people in more ways than can be acknowledged here. Special thanks are due to the following: Linda Auwers, David T. Bailey, Stuart Bruchey, Paul G. E. Clemens, Gerald L. Fetner, Robert W. Gordon, Douglas Greenberg, James A. Henretta, Christopher M. Jedrey, Douglas L. Jones, Stanley N. Katz, Alfred Konefsky, Charles A. Lofgren, Austin Sarat, Donald W. Sutherland, Robert W. Sutherland, Emily Tabuteau, John L. Thomas, G. B. Warden, Robert M. Weir, and Richard White. They have made many valuable suggestions, some of which I have stubbornly resisted. Twenty undergraduates at Michigan State have also contributed to my understanding of colonial American law. They were brave enough to enroll in a seminar on the subject and candid enough to tell me precisely what they thought of the material assigned. I am grateful to them for that advice, and for giving me reason to suppose that a book along these lines might be of interest to students in a liberal arts program.

STEPHEN BOTEIN
East Lansing, Michigan

Contents

Bibliographic Note   127

Essay

Introduction

Before Frederick William Maitland "commanded the dry bones to live," as a close colleague of the great English scholar recalled at the beginning of this century, the legal history of medieval England was "obscure, insulated, a seeming chaos of technical antiquities. Historians excusably shrank from it." Seventeenth- and eighteenth-century American law has never been quite so forbidding a subject, if only because its setting is more recognizable to modern minds. Nevertheless, most historians are disinclined to grapple with its intricate materials, and it has yet to be interpreted by a legal craftsman with Maitland's genius for historically sound simplification.

Scholarship concerned with the legal history of colonial America is apt to strike readers as arcane, especially compared with the literature on the subsequent legal history of the United States. Much of the documentary record has either disappeared or become virtually inaccessible—buried in poorly organized manuscript collections at local archives. Technical terminology abounds in what evidence does survive. And of course the story of early American law lacks a focal institution at the center, such as a Supreme Court trying to resolve urgent public issues by reference to a written national statement of constitutional principles. The ingredients of law in colonial America were mainly English—combined and recombined, often haphazardly, in numerous jurisdictions. Little wonder, then, that a previous generation of scholars tended to dismiss the legal experience of the colonies as mere "frontier" justice rendered in a kind of "dark age" antedating the gloriously "formative" era of American jurisprudence from the Revolution to the Civil War.

1

This misunderstanding of early American law persists in some quarters and encourages historians and students alike to neglect a crucially important element of social reality in the colonial period. Defined broadly, as a body of precepts regulating the relationships of people and property, law was the principal medium through which organized political society operated in the seventeenth and eighteenth centuries. Although government in the American colonies normally conducted its business at minimal expense, without large-scale programs implemented bureaucratically, it was far from light-handed in its efforts to realize public goals. Mostly, it tried to act through the everyday legal regulation of activity that in later times would be regarded as essentially private. By so intervening to guide the behavior and even the beliefs of individuals, the public authorities in colonial America altered the lives of ordinary men and women. The rules of early American law, even when formulated and applied inconsistently, had the effect of recognizing or maintaining the priority of some group interests over others and of strengthening or weakening different patterns of social organization.

Accordingly, almost in spite of themselves, specialized historians of colonial American law have developed some themes that are relevant to major topical concerns of general historical scholarship. Three such themes are worth noting. First, much has been written about the biblical sources of law in seventeenth-century New England—long an obscure subject until a key missing text, the "Laws and Liberties" adopted by Massachusetts in 1648, resurfaced at the turn of the present century. Although the research of legal historians in this area has run parallel to the sophisticated tradition of literary and historical scholarship called "Puritan studies," originating in the 1930s with the brilliant work of Perry Miller, little has been done to interpret the Hebraic laws of early New England within a wider context of religious theory and practice. A second theme in the literature of early American legal history is the relative influence at the local level of English custom and New World circumstances. Here there is a need, now commonly perceived, to integrate the technical analysis of colonial law with recent "community studies," most of which draw selectively on legal records as well as other sources providing economic and demographic data. The town life of colonial New England has been the focus of such inquiry, much as the region's intellectual output has occupied Perry Miller's followers; hence there is also an obvious need to take comparative account of conditions in the middle and southern colonies. Finally, legal historians have shown a continuing interest in the governance of the British Empire, with an emphasis on judicial structures. Specialized research along these lines is still much informed by the "institutional" approach that dominated early American history in the first decades of this century. Charles McLean Andrews and others established this agenda by their minute attention to the wording of colonial charters, English administrative regulations, and the like. Newer scholarship, discussing the "anglicization" of politics and society in the colonies, appears so far to have made only a slight impression on conventional legal historians.

Legal history is relevant to an understanding of early American society, but its potential as a source of basic and unique insight remains unrealized. The purpose of the essay that follows is to sketch out an interpretive framework for thinking about law in relation to other features of colonial America. Chapters 2 and 3 concentrate on two of the three thematic categories mentioned above—law and religion, and law and local society. Each, it will be suggested, helps to identify a distinctive mode of early American legal experience that may be said to reflect characteristic patterns of social thought and action unfolding over two centuries. Most noticeable in this respect are the influence of Nonconformist religion in key sectors of colonial society and the stabilizing effects of tight communal organization. Chapters 1 and 4 adopt the more extended imperial perspective, considering first the imposition of English nationality on the mainland of North America and then the development of transatlantic legal structures. These structures enabled English officials to supervise intercolonial affairs more systematically. The result was intermittent political protest, often localistic in outlook and phrased in the religious language of Nonconformity.

Nothing in the discussion that follows should be understood to imply that the legal elements of early American history were "causes" of the Revolution. Its immediate political origins are too well known to be recited below, and deeper historical explanations lie outside the purview of this essay. Colonial law itself was almost always responsive to broad configurations of social power, as revealed in such circumstances as military strength, population growth, and trade. Without disputing the causal importance of extralegal historical factors, however, it may be argued that law was the effective center of routine colonial politics, where the silent forces of social change made an impact on theories as well as practices of early American government. To some extent, the revolutionary movement of the 1760s and 1770s took the shape it did, generating specific ideas and outcomes, because new imperial policies adopted by the mother country played into a tense context of alternative colonial law that reached back to religious and communal traditions of the previous century. The very ambiguities of early American legal history, which frequently have made the field seem unmanageable, are at the heart of its significance for a full appreciation of the events that culminated in American nationhood.

ONE

A Nation Among Peoples

Two hundred and seventy-five years after John Cabot first saw the coast of Newfoundland, an English population of approximately one and a half million occupied the seaboard region of Northeast America, from Penobscot Bay to Georgia. How this came about, from rudimentary beginnings in Jamestown and Plymouth, is a tale that needs little repeating. Because the process of English colonization was fitful and disorderly, there was much left unclear or unsaid in the record of legal rationalization. Eventually, law was developed both to justify control by this one people of territory in which others claimed rights and to define the status of those who stayed or came to live there under English sovereignty.

The formal theory permitting England's ventures in the New World had none of the lofty sanction that accompanied Spain's. Although paid with Spanish gold, Columbus arrived as "Christ Bearer." In a bull of 1493, a kind of papal charter soon modified by the Treaty of Tordesillas to allow a Portuguese role, Pope Alexander VI donated all "countries and islands . . . hitherto discovered . . . and to be discovered" across the ocean to the king and queen of Spain. They were to rule "in his place" and so in the place of St. Peter, to whom had been entrusted "kingdom and jurisdiction" that included "all the men in the world." This grant was a reward for eight centuries of warfare against the Muslims; it obligated its recipient to promote Christianity among the heathen.

However little such a rationale determined actual Spanish practice, it was a sweepingly thorough statement of legitimacy compared with any advanced by England. Despite frequent reference to the discovery of Newfoundland as the basis of English title in the New World, it was widely acknowledged that "visual apprehension" of territory—even when followed by exploration—established only a flimsy claim. It was flimsier yet because more than half a century elapsed after the first Cabot voyage before anyone in England showed much interest in the possibilities of the American continent. The essence of the English position was an unidealistic argument phrased in language that reflected the rudiments of domestic land law. As Queen Elizabeth explained when the Spanish ambassador presented a complaint about Francis Drake's global expedition of 1577–1580, England flatly refused to "recognize" the authority of the pope to bestow New World territory "as with a fief." Spain had "no claim to property there except that they have established a few settlements and named rivers and capes. . . . Prescription without possession is not valid." So in 1584, Elizabeth gave Sir Walter Raleigh leave to "discover, search, find out, and view" any American lands "not actually possessed by any Christian Prince, nor inhabited by Christian People." Should he encounter such lands, he was entitled to "have, holde, occupie, and enjoy" them.

Precisely what might happen then was difficult to say. The initiatives for the unsuccessful English efforts of the late sixteenth century and the fragile American settlements of later decades came from private groups of adventurers and merchants. Compared with the scope of Roman Catholic involvement elsewhere in the New World, there was little the Church of England could do to shape early colonial policy; and the Crown simply went through the motions of supervising from afar—without providing direct political management or appreciable financial and military support. Legally, there were only the broadest of guidelines. Two model clauses had been formulated for a patent that Sir Humphrey Gilbert, Raleigh's half-brother, had obtained from the queen in 1578, and these were repeated with variations in most patents and charters that followed. According to one, settlers were to retain "all the priviledges" enjoyed by persons "natyve of England and without our allegiance in suche like ample manner and fourme as if they were borne and personally residaunte without our saide realme." Up to a point, this was straightforward enough. English colonists would remain English subjects, and their children born overseas would be English by birthright; as of 1648, the principle seemed so obvious that a bill to that effect in the House of Lords was allowed to languish, as unnecessary. The other clause in Gilbert's patent was fraught with trouble for the future. Granting the power to frame governmental regulations, it stipulated that they be "as neare as conveniently . . . agreable to the forme of the lawes and pollicies of England." Presumably, the meaning of this second clause could well determine the content of that legal birthright envisioned in the first.

Who was to say what was convenient or inconvenient and whether it accorded with English example or interest? This difficult question went unanswered during the first decades of colonization in America, not least because there were "divers lawes within the realme of England"—as the situation was tersely summarized by Sir Edward Coke, the most prominent jurist and legal commentator of the time. While Parliament passed statutes, the royal courts at Westminster developed and applied the special body of jurisprudence known as "common law" and the High Court of Chancery was responsible for another known as "equity." In addition, various ecclesiastical and admiralty and borough and manorial courts handed out enough law of their own that in all Coke had to devise some fifteen different categories to make minimal sense of things. This sprawling legal landscape included no set of precepts to deal specifically with colonial conditions of the sort that evolved on the mainland of North America.

It was generally agreed that English royal authority could be asserted over the inhabitants of "heathen and barbarian lands" in America by reason of conquest in a "just War." This was a convenient doctrine, indirectly confirmed by one of Coke's judicial decisions, but it skirted issues that had been continually ventilated in sixteenth-century Spanish councils. What were the rights of those native Americans whose forebears had discovered the New World many thousands of years before the arrival of Europeans? A cogent dissenting opinion in Spain, argued eloquently from a missionary's point of view by Father Bartolomé de Las Casas, had insisted that papal jurisdiction was spiritual only and that therefore the use of force against natives was unjustified unless they interfered with peaceful preaching. Some Spaniards were also outspoken in rejecting the theory that the Indians of America were suited by their "natural condition" to enslavement. Relatively few Englishmen shared such scruples, however. Perhaps the previous painful experience of trying to colonize the "wild Irish"—separated by a mere channel from the mother country—predisposed many leaders of the first settlements in North America to assume that lawfulness would derive from stark martial imperatives.

"By what right or warrant can we enter into the Land of these Savages," asked one surprisingly candid English promoter in 1609, "take away their rightfull inheritance from them, and plant ourselves in their place, being unwronged or unprovoked by them?" The simplest rationale for dispossession of native Americans was always to cite the fundamental right of self-defense, and this right seemed most compelling when defended against "barbarians" who were said to be capable of gruesome atrocities. It would be "no breach of equitye," as a propagandist for overseas colonization had pointed out in the 1580s, for Christians to "defende themselves, to pursue revenge with force, and to doo whatsoever is necessary for attayning of their safety: For it is allowable by all Lawes in such distresses, to resist violence with violence." Possibly it was disappointing to some impatient settlers, then, that their first contacts with Indians were mostly peaceful. In Virginia, however, the devastating native attack of 1622 put an end to white restraint. The "massacre" was "good for the Plantation," according to the logic of self-defense, because it gave the English "just cause" to "destroy" Indians "by all meanes possible," by "right of Warre, and Law of Nations." There was "nothinge unjust" that might "tend to their ruine."

Especially in the absence of such a violent incident to legitimize relentless warfare, Englishmen were characteristically inclined to buttress proclamations of sovereignty by legal devices or argumentation that purported to establish their property rights in particular North American lands. Most English attempts to acquire territory from native leaders were temporary expedients, often undertaken to rebut claims to title by other Englishmen or by rival European interests. Deceit might well be involved—presentations of "pretty merchaundizes and trifles," along with rum, accompanying promises misrecorded or later broken at will. It was obviously hypocritical to claim, as one Virginian did in 1610, that the English were trading their "pearles of heaven" for the Indians' "pearles of earth." Captain John Smith, temperamentally blunt, said aloud what most of his fellow countrymen must have thought when he informed Opechancanough, Powhatan's half-brother: "You know my want; and I, your plenty: of which, by some means, I must have part."

Here, as in other instances, it was Roger Williams who spoke up as a principled minority of one. Before being banished from the Massachusetts Bay colony in 1635 and then founding Rhode Island on the basis of a grant from a Narragansett chief, Williams contended that Englishmen could have no rights whatsoever in American land unless they secured valid titles from those who had been there first. Trained in law as well as theology, he proceeded to draw the dangerously impolitic conclusion that New Englanders should renounce their patent from the king. This reasoning, it was said, would have "subverted the fundamental State and Government of the Country," and no one else came forward to espouse Williams's views. Even William Penn, sincerely eager in the early 1680s to acquire the land of the Delawares by purchase and so colonize the region with their "Love and Consent," assumed that his authority to be there at all flowed originally from England. "The king of the Countrey where I live," he told tribal negotiators, "hath given me a great Province."

Whether Englishmen adhered in good faith to their own understanding of property rights as they dealt with native tribes was not, in any case, the only issue. Even when they did, or gave the appearance of so doing, they ignored alternative conceptions of property that prevailed among the woodland Indians of the Northeast. Land was thought to have been transmitted by descent from ancestors who had lived and died and been buried in the same area; it belonged to each Indian nation as a whole, not to individuals. In response to the fur trade, it seems, some tribes acknowledged that families might have special interests in particular hunting grounds, but rights to land were inseparable from membership in the community and presupposed continuing participation in the benevolent economy of nature. Tribal or village councils might control certain plots or fields, but no one was authorized to "sell" land according to the sense that Englishmen had of such a transaction. A chief, usually in consultation with his elders, the heads of families, and sometimes representatives of neighboring tribes, might agree to transfer territory to other Indians or to Europeans. This was regarded as a free gift, however, perhaps to facilitate the process of making a fraternal alliance in which each party pledged an effort to meet the other's future needs. One kind of property was not just being exchanged for another of comparable value. Merchandise received during such a voluntary transfer was understood to be a form of ceremonial reciprocity, like the presentation of wampum belts, instead of payment as part of a mutual bargain. European gifts, so interpreted, might then be distributed both within a tribe and without, not as compensation but as a means of recording the deliberations that had taken place. To the bewilderment of most colonial leaders, well-intentioned or not, their native counterparts preferred to rely on oral tradition rather than written documents for proof of previous agreements.

As time passed, tribal negotiators tended to appropriate some elements of English legal language, much as English officials learned to imitate the Indians' rhetorical style (see Documents, pp. 70–74). The marked discrepancy in legal habit between native Americans and Englishmen persisted, however. It not only aggravated misunderstandings on particular occasions but also contributed to a pervasive and derogatory misreading of native American society that in turn reinforced legal justifications for white seizure of land. If not bloodthirsty, the woodland Indians of North America still struck English observers as people who lacked the forms and procedures of civilized political society. It was not on account of heathenism alone that they had to yield to English demands. Scattered population was a tell-tale sign of social inferiority. "If the title of occupiers be good in land unpeopled," Raleigh had asked decades before permanent settlement began in North America, "why should it be bad accounted in a country peopled over thinly?" Such reasoning was elaborated as large-scale migration across the Atlantic became feasible. The natives of New England "inclose noe Land," John Winthrop asserted in 1629 before setting out from the mother country to found the Massachusetts Bay colony, "neither have any settled habitation, nor any tame Cattle to improve the Land by." Surely, those leaving an overpopulated Old World had a right to occupy territory that was scarcely used by the few primitive people already there. The proud and imperious Puritans had a special right to be where they were, since the Lord had directed them to shun corruption in the mother country by fleeing into the "wilderness." Taken to extremes, as it was, this line of argument simply denied that the Indians had ever taken possession of American soil. Because they "roamed," as nomadic hunters, they should no more be allowed to "usurp" the land than wild beasts of the forest.

In fact, as Roger Williams was aware, the economies of the northeastern woodland Indians were at least partially agricultural, although some tribes made regular seasonal moves that gave a misleading impression of impermanency. But realities soon accorded with English doctrine, as Indian populations along the coast succumbed to English disease and force of arms. By 1677, in both the Chesapeake region and New England, violence had set the stage for a final solution of the Indian problem. The previous year, in Virginia, two former students at the Inns of Court in London—Governor William Berkeley and the renegade councilor Nathaniel Bacon—had clashed over issues of Indian policy, the former seeking to protect peaceful natives as subjects of the Crown while the latter urged that all "savages" be "outlawed." In the disastrous course of Bacon's Rebellion, most of the Indians remaining were killed or driven away; a few thousand survivors were rounded up and placed for their own safety on small tracts of reserved land. Almost at the same time, King Philip's War in Massachusetts undermined an experimental Puritan effort to establish a system of semiautonomous villages for Christianized Indians. By the end of the century there was little left of the coastal woodland tribes. The premises of English legal doctrine proved self-verifying, as a quarter of a million colonists displaced a native population of approximately equivalent size.

During the very decades that Englishmen were removing one alien race from their new American territories, they were beginning to import and lay the legal groundwork for enslaving another. Enslavement of Indians had always been a theoretical option, which New Englanders had found particularly easy to rationalize from scriptural sanctions of captivity following a "just War." But in practice there was never much chance of imposing wholesale bondage on tribal groups that were willing either to fight and die together or to retreat quietly into the interior. Nor was it realistic to expect that much could be gained from trying to subjugate people who were so acutely vulnerable to European contagions. On the other hand, there was little to prevent full enslavement of those individual Africans who—at first in small numbers, starting in 1619 with "twenty Negars" reported by John Rolfe to have been purchased from a Dutch man-of-war—entered the Chesapeake region involuntarily. Even so, despite the rapid introduction of black chattel slavery in the British West Indies, it took the mainland tobacco colonies more than four decades to decide unequivocally to write such a labor system into law. One reason for this delay, it seems, was that Englishmen needed that much experience to appreciate why enslaving blacks was possibly the best way to avoid the worst consequences of having to restrict the freedom of their own countrymen.

Such restriction was temporary, to be sure, but still degrading. For most of the seventeenth century, the great majority of field hands working in gangs in the tobacco fields of the Chesapeake region were white indentured servants from the mother country. Many were young and poor, sometimes having been forced or induced by fraud to board a ship for the New World. If they had signed their indentures in England, in exchange for ocean passage under miserably crowded and unsanitary conditions, they would then be sold on arrival for the period of service specified in their contracts—anywhere from one or two to seven years or more. At the end they could set out on their own, with some clothing and tools as "freedom dues" and perhaps an official grant of acreage. Indentured servants were unqualified to vote, engage in trade, or marry without the consent of their masters. Most important, their obligation of service was transferable. Servants in Virginia, according to one English merchant, "were sold . . . up and down like horses." In 1633, a Dutch sea captain discovered a group of local planters gambling at cards with their servants as stakes. Understandably, a servant might feel that he or she was being treated "like a damnd slave." One, duped into an extraordinary fifteen-year term of service in Maryland, successfully petitioned the governor and Council for relief because it was "contrary to the laws of God and man that a Christian subject should be made a slave."

There was no legal analogue in the mother country to the colonial institution of white servitude. Servants in England normally signed annual contracts, which were made under constabulary supervision at large open labor markets and required three months' notice by either party if they were not to be renewed. Apprenticeship agreements for the young lasted longer and imposed rigid restrictions on personal freedom, but they were not freely transferable from master to master. Indentured service was effective in moving people to the New World to meet a growing demand for labor, especially in the Chesapeake colonies; but how could English settlers hope to prosper if they continued systematically to reduce their own people to a condition that John Rolfe agreed would have been "most intolerable" in the mother country? The irony of the situation pointed toward an effort to distinguish and degrade the status of black labor.

Before midcentury, there were some Africans in the Chesapeake colonies who evidently served for life, with the same obligation passing to their children; others worked with and on the same terms as white servants or were free. Gradually, the position of blacks deteriorated. More and more transactions were recorded that unambiguously defined what slavery was coming to mean in colonial America—as in 1652, when a planter in Virginia sold a ten-year-old black girl "with her Issue and produce duringe her (or either of them) for their Life tyme" and "their Successors forever." White servants, it was emphasized by way of contrast, would serve for their "full terme of tyme" only. Over several decades following 1660, a miscellaneous assortment of statutes appeared on the books in Maryland, as well as in Virginia, that had the effect of recognizing and regularizing these practices. In language that was often imprecise and inconsistent, Chesapeake legislators moved toward codification of the formula that all blacks and no whites would be slaves "Durante Vita" (see Documents, pp. 74–75). Baptism would no longer imply any possibility of freedom; miscegenation, the issue of which were both "abominable" in racial terms and "spurious" in their legal status, was banned. A slave was just another asset, attachable for debts and liable for purposes of taxation. Virginia, in 1705, declared slaves to be the equivalent of real estate and therefore subject to the usual rules of inheritance. At the same time, the right of servants to own a few animals or other such minor property was affirmed. White indentured servitude might be harsh, but surely it was not slavery.

Nothing comparable to the latter system existed in England, although certainly not for lack of racial prejudice. If black slavery in the colonies helped English servants there feel some residual sense of participation in their national heritage, despite the rigors of their position, it was also a huge and troubling anomaly that the conventional legal wisdom of the mother country could not comprehend. In 1661, Virginia had expressly adopted the whole of English law except where "a difference of condition" made it inapplicable. English law suited a population that was more or less homogeneous, however, whereas at least some colonies were beginning to absorb markedly different peoples. In the following century, when finally there was some sustained program to regulate colonial affairs from the mother country, the curious legal consequences of racial and ethnic diversity in the swelling population of mainland America became more obvious.

New York's Dutch inhabitants posed difficulties. England had never recognized Dutch sovereignty there and in any case could readily justify royal transformation of the New Netherlands after 1664 by right of conquest; but in practice this took time to achieve. For several decades, in the interest of conciliating a sullen local majority, English courts allowed Dutch residents to retain their own customs concerning inheritance and to settle contracts made before 1664 according to Roman civil usages observed in the New Netherlands. The new Mayor's Court of the City of New York operated, for a time, much like New Amsterdam's old Court of Burgomaster, Schepens and Schout, and Dutch "burgher-right" was respected as the basis of local citizenship. Subsequently, as English settlers poured into the colony, it became feasible to suppress most Dutch forms, but not without encountering stubborn resistance that continued through the eighteenth century. Although as a group the Dutch of New York committed relatively few crimes, they were in the habit of flouting the English polity. One Dutch official in Dutchess County, more audacious than most, was heard to have said that he "Valued no English Law no more than a Turd."

If the Dutch could be vexing, other whites entering the colonies in the eighteenth century seemed nearly ungovernable. Immigrants from Ulster in Northern Ireland, the Presbyterian Scotch-Irish, were traditionally hostile to English authority, having previously suffered both religious and commercial discrimination by parliamentary statute. Streaming through the back country of the middle and southern colonies, they were welcomed for their ability to clear land and guard the frontier, but they impressed Englishmen as a "vicious" people of warring clans. Indifferent to jurisdictional boundaries and English legal conventions, they often squatted on whatever vacant land appealed to them. In 1730, according to a report sent back to the mother country by a proprietary agent, one group of Scotch-Irish in Pennsylvania had settled in a "disorderly manner" on some fifteen thousand acres reserved to the Penn family. By way of explanation, they said that "it was against the laws of God and nature that so much land should be idle when so many Christians wanted it to labor on and to raise their bread."

German-speaking immigrants from the Palatine also arrived in large numbers during the eighteenth century, to spread out through the back country south of New England. Although their reputation among the English was less unsavory than that of the Scotch-Irish, they included numerous pietistic sects—Mennonites, Dunkers, Schwenkfelders, Moravians—espousing various degrees of nonaccommodation with civil government. Further, coming as they did from the Continent, their legal status as subjects or citizens was unclear. In theory, they could be declared citizens of the realm either by what was called a royal patent of "denization" or by a parliamentary naturalization act, but these were expensive individualized procedures that required considerable political sophistication. Some colonial governors and assemblies devised less costly and intricate means of conferring a kind of local citizenship on the new arrivals. These arrangements lacked uniformity, however, and were of dubious legality from an English point of view.

In 1740, trying to clarify the situation, Parliament passed a general act that allowed foreign settlers in the colonies to acquire certificates of naturalization valid in all parts of the empire after seven years of residence. Brief absences were permitted by this legislation, the costs of application were minimal, and there were some exemptions from its requirement of avowed Protestantism. In the next three decades, however, fewer than seven thousand colonists were naturalized accordingly. A smaller number continued to take advantage of older local laws on the books—until 1773, when these were flatly prohibited by the Privy Council in London. English law might be liberal, but it was remote as well. And seven years could be an inconveniently long time to have to be classified as an alien, whose land would revert to the government in case of death. Many of the new immigrants were not indentured but redemptioner servants, which meant that they had paid part of their passage before departure and could often therefore manage to discharge the rest of their obligation quickly. If their transactions in land turned out to be open to legal challenge, general security of title might be seriously unsettled (see Documents, pp. 75–79). From the perspective of the mother country, however, the Privy Council saw no reason to countenance local legislative attempts to provide a measure of relief.

So in the course of the eighteenth century, English law proved less than adequate for effective regulation of an increasingly diversified white population on the colonial mainland. South of New England, there were vast expanses of territory beyond the reach of coastal officialdom where settlers of varied ethnic and religious backgrounds simply had to make do in the absence of an effective sovereign state. The most conspicuous failure in this regard was the colony of South

Carolina, which supplied no judicial service at all outside the port town of Charleston. Eighteenth-century England itself still included small pockets of people outside the law, most of them located in forest districts that agents of the Crown were striving to bring under control. By comparison, the situation in several colonial jurisdictions appeared anarchic. The majority of whites in some areas remained as uncolonized as the majority of people inhabiting the far west of Ireland.

Meanwhile, the number of black slaves in the colonies was growing prodigiously, well beyond what anyone had foreseen when the new system of labor first took statutory form. By midcentury slavery was firmly established in some northern colonies and accounted for at least one third of the total population from Maryland southward, where the economics of staple agricultural production had combined decisively with English racial attitudes to shift the balance in favor of perpetually unfree labor. One result, particularly in areas where whites were not numerous enough to feel safe, was an immense volume of legislation to keep blacks in order. Special courts were erected to try slaves accused of committing felonies, according to rules of evidence that differed from English practice; special patrols were authorized to protect the countryside, sometimes with extraordinary powers of search and seizure in slave quarters; special punishments were decreed for slaves, and special regulations governed their movements. Slavery was no longer just an anomaly in English law. It was itself a separate legal system within the framework of empire.

Finally, there were more Indians to contend with, not along the coast but toward the interior—where large and well-organized tribes could engage in resistance to white encroachment by adept maneuvering among rival European nations. This political reality, in turn, vastly complicated official handling of legal disputes within the colonies that involved long-dormant Indian claims to land. Sir William Johnson, royal superintendent of Indian Affairs, explained candidly in 1765 that it was his "invariable rule" to avoid questioning "old Titles of his Majestys Subjects" when challenged by a "domesticated" tribe of "little consequence or importance to his Majestys interest." On the other hand, in the case of a "Just complaint made by a People either by themselves or Connections capable of resenting . . . a neglect," he would elect to "support the same, although it disturb the property of any Man whatsoever."

Here, as in many circumstances, the difficult task of determining what English law applied in the colonies was magnified by the presence of non-English peoples there. By the middle of the eighteenth century, for political purposes that had nothing to do with Indian policy, some ethnocentric English statesmen on opposite sides of the Atlantic were disposed to affirm the theoretical supremacy of English law in the colonies by means of a doctrine that incidentally denied the historical existence of the very people who were stirring up the frontier. England had not "conquered" America, it was maintained, but had "discovered" territories there that were "vacant." This was significant because all English law, according to one much-admired judicial dictum, was automatically in force in uninhabited lands newly found by Englishmen. Thus the colonies were fully part of the English legal system from the beginning; the first settlers had carried with them the entire polity of the mother country as their inheritance. The logic of seventeenth-century doctrine and events was at last complete. The problem of native American rights had disappeared (see Documents, pp. 79–82).

This was an elegant formulation, but ultimately unrealistic. Apart from sweeping aside not only Indians but blacks, Palatines, Scotch-Irish, and others with different legal birthrights, it ignored emerging disagreements among Englishmen themselves as to what it meant to live within the realm. Not least because the colonies had become far less English than the mother country, it was less satisfactory than ever to rely on the vague formulas of the first royal patents and charters. A century and a half after the founding of Jamestown, it appeared that the "lawes and pollicies" of the mother country and those of her mainland colonies could not "conveniently" be made as "agreable" as proponents of unitary English nationhood assumed.

TWO

Religion and the State

Within the general legal environment that English settlers tried to establish in northeastern America, perhaps the most important ideological source of disharmony was religion. At the extremes of the colonial Protestant spectrum were strict advocates of the Church of England as a state religion and radical dissenters espousing pure voluntarism. In most places at most times, however, the legal issues dividing colonists as they went about organizing their ecclesiastical affairs were more subtle. What developed eventually was a troublesome pattern of localistic deviation from English norms. The precarious role of the Church of England in colonial America was symptomatic of underlying weaknesses in the structure of transatlantic empire.

Despite ritual declarations by clergymen in late seventeenth-century New England that the colonies of their region had originated as "plantations of religion"—in contrast to the "plantations of trade" founded in the Chesapeake area—there is no reason to think that the Puritans monopolized official religiosity during the early years of settlement. In Virginia, it was taken for granted from the start that public authority had a major function to perform in collaborating with the Church to supervise moral conduct throughout the territorial boundaries of its jurisdiction and to maintain uniformity of belief. Even in the brutal early days of Sir Thomas Dale's Code, residents of Jamestown were governed by "Divine" and "Moral" as well as "Martial" regulations. Twice a day, by drumbeat, they marched to prayers; severe penalties were prescribed for nonattendance and profanity. Then, in 1619, the first colonial Assembly passed a series of laws against gaming, drunkenness, swearing, and other moral offenses, authorizing both clergymen and civil officials to discipline those guilty of such "ungodly disorders" (see Documents, pp. 82–85). As late as 1705, the legislature in Virginia was still busy attempting to enforce observance of the Sabbath. Maryland, in 1678, drew up the usual laws to curb the "wicked and profane licentiousness" of its inhabitants. Somewhat later an acting governor there, representing a Catholic proprietor, pronounced drunkenness to be "a sin of all sins"—although presumably not as bad as adultery, which this same official wanted to define as a capital crime. With the colony under royal control, another governor urged members of the Assembly to go back to their counties and implement "all the good Laws against Sabbathbreaking, Prophane Cursing and Swearing, Adultery, and fornication, etc." In New York, much the same set of concerns underlay "An Act for Suppressing Immorality" passed by the General Assembly in 1708, which prescribed harsh penalties and was accompanied by an exhortatory preamble.

Although the colonies south of New England followed traditional Elizabethan theory in writing laws to criminalize sin and encourage righteousness, they failed to replicate the Anglican ecclesiastical system that had been largely responsible for such legal regulation in the mother country. The Church of England did not help matters along by trying to govern colonial religious institutions out of the bishopric of London instead of creating a diocese in the New World. But it appears that most colonial Anglicans had no great enthusiasm for closer supervision, and anyway the circumstances of their local religious life argued against importing a full state establishment.

The case of Virginia is most revealing in this respect, although variations on problems encountered there were common in other colonies. Without a resident bishop to ordain and install ministers, and without land of high rental value to support them, Anglicans in Virginia soon learned to make do with a clergy insufficient in numbers to serve every parish and recruited from the least competent ranks of the church in the mother country. To spread the burden of maintaining this clergy among dispersed planters, parish boundaries might extend as far as fifty miles. The result was a local breakdown of hierarchical structures in the church. Vestrymen struggled successfully with the governor of the colony for the right to choose new ministers for vacant parishes. In 1664, heeding royal instructions to preserve the traditional forms of Anglicanism "as near as may be," the General Assembly insisted that all ceremonies and rites "be according to the orders and canons of England, and the Sacraments . . . performed according to the Book of Common Prayer." Since this was inconvenient, given the size of parishes and the condition of the clergy, lay Anglicans continued to bury their dead in unconsecrated family graveyards, perform marriages on their own, and otherwise depart from proper ecclesiastical procedure. And like colonial Anglicans everywhere, they declined to erect a system of ecclesiastical courts.

These ancient tribunals, which claimed almost exclusive jurisdiction over such matters as marriage and sexual behavior in addition to church doctrine and administration, were little esteemed in the mother country—least of all by Puritans. Many Englishmen complained both of their laxity in enforcing morals and of their cruel antagonism toward dissidents. Abolished during the political upheavals of the 1640s, they were subsequently reinstated but without as much effective power. Toward the end of the seventeenth century, an official of the Church of England, James Blair, arrived in Virginia with limited authority to manage ecclesiastical affairs. In 1690, at his instigation, a convention of the colony's ministers approved a plan to introduce ecclesiastical courts for the purpose of disciplining "all cursers Swearers and blasphemers, all whoremongers fornicators and Adulterers, all drunkards ranters and profaners of the Lords day." Although Blair would soon join the governor's Council, he was never able to win wide support for his proposal, which was said to have "terrified" ordinary Virginians.

Apparently they preferred to retain the lay-controlled system of moral regulation that had been developed in a series of colonial statutes around midcentury. Local vestrymen would choose churchwardens, who were charged with inquiring into the morals of the parish and presenting written reports of their findings twice a year to the appropriate county court. In cases of deliquency, the vestry itself might hear evidence and take depositions, but prosecutions—even if managed by a churchwarden—would be brought before the county justices. Although often serving as vestrymen too, the justices handled moral offenses as officials of the state; their judgments, which commonly involved fines or whippings or public confessions in church, might be executed by either a sheriff or a churchwarden. Such procedures, characteristic of Maryland and

New York as well, jumbled civil and ecclesiastical government, but they firmly established the laity's authority to oversee morals.

The net effect was irregular enforcement, depending on the temper of the local leaders who dominated both vestries and courts. Everyone knew that a clergyman in Virginia, always in doubt whether his contract would be renewed, was not going to denounce the "Vices that any great Man of the Vestry was guilty of." But vestrymen themselves, however righteous, appear to have been reluctant to look very closely into the sins of their neighbors. In the absence of a confession, two witnesses were needed to sustain such serious charges as fornication and adultery. Informants were discouraged from coming forward, since they were liable for court costs in the event of acquittal, and accusations of grave delinquency were as likely to result in successful defamation suits as in convictions. A statute of 1662, specifying punishments for those who spread groundless rumors that disturbed the peace, indicated that planters in the Chesapeake region found it most convenient to live their own lives and let others do the same. Evidently it was this philosophy, rather than skepticism regarding the occult, that underlay the pronounced tendency of Chesapeake courts to treat charges of witchcraft as actionable "slander and scandall" without bothering to try the accused.

A similar pattern of prudent inattention characterized the response of local officialdom to the arrival of Quakers in seventeenth-century Virginia. Despite stern threats by Governor Berkeley and a sequence of explicit if relatively mild penal statutes, there was much de facto tolerance of Quakers at the county level. Sometimes they were harassed by prosecutions for failure to attend church as required by law, but on other occasions their very antipathy toward ecclesiastical authority was echoed sympathetically in local courtrooms. In 1650, for example, a grand jury in Lower Norfolk County dramatically charged the entire population with breach of the Sabbath and then proceeded to blame this deplorable situation on the clergy. The Quaker outlook, so vigorously anticlerical, was not altogether strange in a colony that had failed to import the institutional apparatus of Anglicanism.

Established state religion in Virginia declined further during the eighteenth century, to a point where many traditionalists were tempted to look outside the Church of England for spiritual leadership. While prosecutions for swearing and similar offenses might be numerous in some counties, a statute of 1727 imposing fines on householders who neglected to report bastards born in their homes was a sign that the legal enforcement of morality had become quite languid in others. So had the legal enforcement of religious uniformity. To encourage settlement along the frontier, the House of Burgesses passed miscellaneous acts exempting foreign Protestants from parish levies. After 1740, as the religious fervor of the Great Awakening swept through the colony, dissenting itinerants preached to enthusiastic crowds in defiance of restrictive regulations. The commissary of the Church of England warned "lest their Insolence sh'd grow to a *dangerous* Height," but official harrassment only seemed to intensify their zeal. Appearing in the 1750s, Baptist spokesmen were sharply critical of lapses in virtue by local justices of the peace as well as by the established clergy.

In 1755, when Anglican ministers in the colony petitioned for higher salaries, the House of Burgesses was almost unanimous in rejecting their request; instead, Virginia's Two-Penny Act fixed the ratio of tobacco to currency in such a way as to reduce clerical income drastically. This, according to an address of ten angry clergymen to the bishop of London, was both "a breaking in upon our establishment" and "an insult to the Royal Prerogative." Another such Two-Penny Act, passed in 1758, was eventually disallowed by the Privy Council in London—Virginia's governor having been too mindful of what would "please the people" to veto it. Here was the setting for the celebrated "Parson's Cause" of 1763, on the eve of the revolutionary era, in which the twenty-three-year-old Patrick Henry persuaded a jury to award only nominal damages to a minister suing for the back pay due him. Henry's argument, radical in its constitutional implications, questioned whether the Crown could legitimately place the interests of the clergy over a "law of general utility." It was clear that the English model of official state religion had not prevailed in Virginia.

The English model certainly had influenced other colonies no more, and usually less. Such eighteenth-century Anglican jurisdictions as South Carolina, Maryland, and New York included so many dissenters of English as well as other ethnic origin that it would have been foolhardy to try to compel adherence to a state church. The old Carolina charter of 1663 had recognized the need for indulgence of dissent, in spite of the "unity and uniformity established in this nation," because it was essential to attract as many settlers as possible; among those who later emigrated, earnest Anglicans were an embattled minority. In any case, traditional supervision of morality had to be negligible in a colony that failed not only to create ecclesiastical courts but to deliver even secular justice outside its capital town. Conditions further north were less chaotic yet still unfavorable to the cause of Anglican orthodoxy. "Here bee not many of the Church of England," New York's Governor Thomas Dongan had reported to London in 1687. In the middle of the next century there were not enough to overcome a determined Presbyterian campaign against their plan to organize King's College—later Columbia—as a publicly supported Anglican institution (see Documents, pp. 85–89).

Two other colonies, Pennsylvania and Rhode Island, were committed to religious tolerance by the ideological preferences of their founders. In the former, Quaker hopes for moral reformation were to be realized not through the state at all but in the voluntary discipline of their local and monthly meetings, which followed procedures dictated by the "Gospel Order" of the New Testament in regulating the personal behavior of members and even in settling commercial disputes. Eventually, because so many noncompliant Quakers had to be "disowned," this utopian system proved less workable than the ordinary processes of civil justice backed up by the coercive powers of government. The experimental operation of Quaker moral law for several decades, however, testified to the strength of a radical religious vision that acknowledged the necessity of the state as a basis of external social control but looked elsewhere for enhancement of the inner life. This was an ideal that Rhode Island's Roger Williams had expounded in a sophisticated theological dialogue with the leadership of Massachusetts Bay. His reasoning was that Anti-Christ, in the form of the Roman Catholic papacy, had fulfilled prophecy by extinguishing the true church. There was no apostolic line of continuity to link modern Christians to Hebraic examples of religious lawmaking. As Williams understood the meaning of Christian history, then, it was no longer justifiable for government to lay claim to any jurisdiction beyond "the bodies and goods and outward state of men," although in that limited sphere it might well be severely repressive.

This was a proposition that met with favor among many English dissenters, who considered Williams an outstanding statesman of the New World. Most Puritans in New England, however, responded to the challenges of the frontier by trying to stake out a middle way of their own. Theirs was an ambiguous theory, susceptible to different readings and applications. If conformable to "rules gathered from the word of God, and the clear light of nature in civil nations," it was explained in the preamble to the Massachusetts code of 1648, "surely there is no humane law that tendeth to common good . . . but the same is mediately a law of God, and that in way of an Ordinance which all are to submit unto and that for conscience sake." Further, government and organized religion might properly collaborate— "whereby each do help and strengthen other (the Churches the civil Authorities, and the civil Authorities the Churches.)" Somehow, this had to be done without violating the principle of congregational autonomy. That same year, while granting the right of the state to enforce obedience "in matters of godliness," the Cambridge Platform of Church Discipline pronounced it to be as "unlawfull" for "the Magistrate to meddle with the work proper to church-officers" as for "church-officers to meddle with the sword of the magistrate."

The legal consequences of such delicately nuanced doctrine were various. Puritans in New England were perhaps most faithful to their intellectual origins in their provisions for congregational discipline of those members who transgressed scriptural laws against such offenses as drunkenness, unchastity, cheating, and heresy. Much as the Quakers later did in Pennsylvania, they tried and sometimes excommunicated offenders, although they tended to stop short of that extreme penalty in hopes of restoration, and they were less inclined to attempt to resolve issues that arose in ordinary business dealings. A Puritan church might appoint a standing committee to prepare cases; decisions were made by majority vote and proclaimed by the minister. It was true that nothing could be done if—as once happened in Quincy, Massachusetts—a sinner simply turned his back and walked out the door while his pastor was warming to the usual exhortation, but it seems that congregational reprimand was a grave matter to more pious men. Robert Keayne, the Boston merchant who in 1639 was admonished by his church for taking excessive profits, conceded years afterward that such a judgment "from God . . . was most just." Having also been convicted and fined by a civil court for the same offense, he saw no reason to agree that "the censure was just and righteous from men." The latter judgment was unavoidable because it carried with it the power of the state, but only the former compelled assent from Keayne's conscience.

Such double jeopardy was not uncommon in Massachusetts, since the disciplinary verdicts of a congregation had no civil consequences and most colonial Puritans thought the deterrents of secular law could be helpful in persuading men and women to turn from sin toward righteousness. It was quite atypical to maintain, as some Puritans on Long Island would later, that such offenses as fornication and profanity were merely "cognizable in a Spirituall Court." The prevalent assumption was reflected in a Massachusetts statute of 1665, which denounced fornication as not only a "shameful Sin" but also a "particular Crime"—"much increasing amongst us, to the great dishonour of God, and our Profession of his Holy Name." As in seventeenth-century Virginia, so in most of Puritan New England, morality was an important component of statutory law. But there were significant differences. The Puritans separated religious and civil authority by formally distinguishing congregational discipline from the operations of secular courts; and they sought to implement Hebraic standards of justice that were peculiarly appropriate to their self-image as a latter-day "chosen People" or "second Israel."

Except for Roger Williams's Rhode Island, where English law was said to apply in the absence of local enactments, the ideal polity of early Puritan New England was thought to comprehend divine intentions as revealed in Mosaic law. This was natural enough when such colonial founding fathers as Thomas Hooker of Hartford and John Davenport of New Haven were themselves clergymen who believed that "the practice of the Jewish Church directed by God" embodied "a perfect rule for the . . . government of all men in all duties." Statements to this effect sometimes meant only that legal precepts found in the Old Testament might serve as general guidelines for policy—"till they be branched out in particular hereafter." But there was no mistaking the specific biblical sources of some statutory law in Massachusetts. Although ministers could not act as public officials there, they advised lawmakers from time to time and so had a substantial say in the legal affairs of the colony. In 1636, at the request of legislators eager to lay the groundwork for an infant jurisdiction, John Cotton had drawn up a code known as "Moses his Judicialls." This was not adopted, but some of its Hebraic content resurfaced in the "Body of Liberties" formulated in 1641 by another minister, Nathaniel Ward, who had also been trained as a lawyer in the mother country. Technically, it seems, Ward's code was never enacted, in order to avoid the appearance of disharmony with English law. Many of its provisions were recycled into the "Laws and Liberties" of 1648, however, which influenced legislation in Connecticut, New Hampshire, and to a lesser extent New York, New Jersey, and Pennsylvania. Especially in the text of Massachusetts's notorious "Capital lawes," which prescribed death for such offenses as adultery and the cursing or smiting of parents, scriptural citations appeared by way of authoritative explanation. The Old Testament thus provided Puritans with a special legal vocabulary upon which they could draw selectively to achieve their mission of constructing a holy commonwealth. In this as well as other respects, local dissidents led by Dr. Robert Child had been correct when they accused the Bay colony in 1646 of deviating from what they referred to as the "Fundamental and wholesome Lawes" of England. To this charge the General Court had replied evasively, pointing out "Parallels" between Puritan and English law but nevertheless insisting that such conformity was not required and that justice in Massachusetts would be dispensed "according to the word of God."

Practice was less exacting than theory in New England, but still far from light-handed. In Plymouth, a young man named Thomas Granger experienced the full rigor of Mosaic justice when in 1642 he was indicted for "buggery . . . with a mare, a cowe, tow goats, five sheep, 2 calves, and a turkey." Having confessed, he was condemned to die. "A very sade spectakle it was," observed Governor William Bradford; "for first the mare, and then the cowe, and the rest of the lesser catle, were kild before his face, according to the law, Levit: 20.15 and then he him selfe was executed. The catle were all cast into a great & large pitte . . . , and no use made of any part of them." Unlike the Chesapeake region, early New England was a land where "wickedness" was "much witnessed against," as Bradford noted, ". . . and narrowly looked unto, & severely punished when it was knowne." The preamble to the "Laws and Liberties" of 1648 quoted approvingly that "old and true proverb" that "the execution of the law is the life of the law." Although no one was ever sentenced to death for abuse of a parent, Puritans generally tried to emulate the example of Calvinist Geneva by following through on charges against minor as well as serious offenders, seeking full substantiation and then prosecuting to a definitive conclusion. High rates of conviction and low rates of acquittal were typical of courts in Puritan communities. This was so not just in New England but also in a colony such as

New York, where rigorous moral regulation in one heavily Puritan county contrasted sharply with lax procedures elsewhere.

Further, despite a stipulation in the "Laws and Liberties" that "no humane power be Lord over the Faith and Consciences of men," seventeenth-century Massachusetts was appreciably stricter than Virginia in controlling ecclesiastical life. In addition to standard laws that associated political rights with church membership, imposed fines for absence from services without reason, and punished contemptuous behavior toward the clergy, the public authorities were quick to frame legislation aimed at suppressing such deviant religious groups as Anne Hutchinson and her followers in the 1630s and the Quakers who invaded the region in the 1650s. Writing in 1645, Nathaniel Ward expressed disdain for "laxe Tolerations upon State-pretences and planting necessities," as exemplified in other colonies. "Experience will teach Churches and Christians," he predicted, "that it is farre better to live in a State united, though somewhat Corrupt, than in a State, whereof some Part is Incorrupt, and all the rest divided." This was the language of territorial religious establishment.

Gradually, the Puritan identity of early New England eroded. A new royal charter issued in 1691 forced Massachusetts to abandon much of the idiosyncratic biblicism and intolerance that had informed its previous laws. And reaction to the witchcraft prosecutions of 1692, which by no means contradicted norms of legal procedure to the extent that legend has made out, indicated the emergence of powerful local leaders who were hesitant to pursue "wickedness" with the vigor of former times (see Documents, pp. 89–94). Still, the old middle way of colonial Puritanism endured, with many of the same ambiguities that had troubled the first generation and some new ones as well. Blasphemy and sexual offenses continued to bulk large among the crimes for which New Englanders were punished, although for the latter category the trend by the middle of the eighteenth century was to concentrate on instances where bastard children threatened local taxpayers with the economic burden of public maintenance. In some communities, despite a proliferation of sectarian controversy, congregations went on trying to enforce the rule of harmony among members.

If the state no longer banished dissidents, it did its best to support religious uniformity by public taxation for the support of orthodox clergymen. Originally some Puritans had been embarrassed at having to resort to such a system, which smacked of popery. But Cotton Mather was unapologetic on behalf of his clerical brethren when he argued, in 1726, that the public rate in Massachusetts was imposed with the tacit approval of the king and therefore might be considered a royal levy. "In Consequence of this," he concluded triumphantly, "the *Minister* . . . is (not only CHRIST'S, but also) in Reality, *The King's Minister*. And the *Salary* raised for him, is raised in the *King's* Name, and is the *King's* Allowance unto him." A clergyman in Virginia could have wished only to claim as much. Indeed, bringing political pressure to bear from London, Anglicans as well as Quakers and Baptists in Massachusetts and Connecticut were shrewd enough to extract statutory concessions that earmarked their tax money for the maintenance of their own ministers. The fact remained, as Cotton Mather's father had boasted at the turn of the century, that "Conformists" in New England were "Dissenters" while "Nonconformists" of Puritan background dominated government.

Their sway was particularly oppressive in Connecticut, which had managed to retain its independent corporate charter. The Saybrook Platform was adopted there in 1708, to facilitate cooperation between church councils and the state in supervising individual congregations. In 1742–1743, following the first revivalistic uproars of the Great Awakening, Connecticut passed a group of statutes known as the "Intolerant Acts." Aimed at Separatists who in the name of a higher orthodoxy directly questioned the spiritual leadership of the colony's clerical establishment, this elaborately detailed legislation regulated the comings and goings of preachers, penalized offenders or ordered their transportation out of the colony, disallowed marriages and baptisms that they had performed, removed their sympathizers from civil office, and tightened doctrinal control of educational institutions. So uncompromising was the repression in Connecticut that Benjamin Avery, chief spokesman for the "Dissenting Interest" in London, was moved to object. "Wee cannot be of Opinion," he wrote to Governor Jonathan Law, "that the Magistrate has any thing to do in this matter; but to see that the publick peace is preserved." This made no impression, and fifteen years later Avery was still vainly laboring to persuade the authorities in Connecticut that "civil penalties were not the appropriate remedy for spiritual disorders."

Opposition to local establishment was also growing inside New England. Except among the entrenched clergy of Connecticut and their allies, it was becoming ever more apparent to New Englanders—

"from the Make of Humane Nature, itself," as their dissenting friends in the mother country liked to say—that mankind would persist in differing on points of religion. Caustically surveying the religious life of the region at midcentury, President Thomas Clap of Yale identified a "New Scheme" by which it was proposed that "every Man" had a "Right to judge *for himself*." This originated in neither the radical religious vision that had animated Roger Williams nor the kind of lay anticlericalism that was so pervasive in Virginia. Its basis was the contractual model of social thought associated with the name of John Locke, as transmitted by religious figures of various persuasions in New England. Connecticut's Elisha Williams, a lawyer and judge who had also been ordained as a clergyman, pleaded the cause of the Great Awakening in 1744 by affirming the "essential Rights and Liberties of Protestants." The "*Right of private Judgment*, and *worshipping* GOD according to their *Consciences*," he argued, was a "*natural and unalienable Right* . . ., what men by entering into civil Society neither did, nor could give up into the Hands of the Community." More specifically, a Separatist clergyman might justify withdrawal from an established church on the grounds that its regular pastor had neglected to fulfill the duties expected of him by those who had promised obedience in the fundamental "covenant" of the congregation (see Documents, pp. 94–98). From a different perspective, such an arch opponent of the Awakening in the Boston area as Charles Chauncy was certain that "the use of Force, in Matters of Religion and Conscience, is not only contrary to the *Example of Christ*, and the *Precepts of his Gospel*; but to the *Nature and Reason of Things*." Jonathan Mayhew, a younger clerical colleague who was in close touch with London's dissenting circles, told the governor and General Court of Massachusetts that a "neighboring colony" had seen fit to enact "some laws of the persecuting aspect," which were in no way "reconcilable" with the temper of the times.

Soon enough, as Anglicans in New England mounted an aggressive campaign to propagandize the region and increase their numbers, Chauncy and Mayhew would lead a counteroffensive calling for comprehensive disestablishment of the empire. There was "no ground for controversy," proclaimed Mayhew in 1763, that Protestants "in any part of his Majesty's dominions" were entitled "to worship God in their own way respectively, without molestation." Anglicans, therefore, had to renounce what Mayhew perceived as their "formal design to dissolve and root out all our New-England churches; or, in other words, to reduce them all to the episcopal form." Skipping lightly over "some instances of unjustifiable severity" by early Puritans, Mayhew suggested that the "Fore-fathers" of the region "would have had no occasion to take refuge" there had they been accorded "liberty of conscience" in the mother country.

Here, just before the imperial crisis that led to American independence, was a challenge to the Church of England even more sweeping than that voiced the same year in Virginia by Patrick Henry. If Christianity was "part of the laws of England," as Americans could shortly read in a colonial edition of William Blackstone's *Commentaries*, there was no escaping the truth that this precept applied differently in the New World than in the mother country. Nor could religious differences among English colonists themselves be easily ignored. It was ironic that state-sponsored churches were most powerful in an old Puritan stronghold such as Connecticut, whereas Anglicanism was under attack almost everywhere. This curiously untraditional pattern of conflict had come about slowly within an ideological context shaped by the novel and irregular features of colonial American society.

THREE

Community and Conflict

The development of early American law was influenced not only by various experiments in ecclesiastical organization that weakened or competed with the Church of England, but also by the pressures of narrowly localized social experience in colonies that had been formed without steady direction from the mother country. In some areas, especially through the network of small towns that dotted New England, the result was a consensual mode of lawmaking that survived under stress into the eighteenth century. Elsewhere, in the absence of cohesive communities, law tended to become an instrument by which a parochial-minded gentry class could attempt to exploit people who had little or no access to political power. Neither of these configurations enhanced imperial authority.

Some early Puritan leaders at first resisted efforts to organize the local polity into a system emphasizing official accountability and popular participation. Foremost of these was John Winthrop, whose long governorship of Massachusetts was disturbed repeatedly by disputes concerning the legitimacy of executive power. A thoughtful student of theology, like so many of the Puritan laity, Winthrop was knowledgeable as well in law, having served as an attorney in an English court that supervised wardships. In July of 1645, after being acquitted at an impeachment trial for exceeding his responsibilities as a magistrate, he made a speech to the General Court of the Bay colony that set forth the essentials of his political theory. "It is yourselves who have called us to this office," he said, "and being called by you, we have our authority from God." The "covenant" underlying this relationship, according to Winthrop, required "faithfulness" on his part without stipulating any particular degree of "skill and ability." Only in the event of bad faith involving violation of principles basic to his official oath was removal of a magistrate justified, and only then if the transgression was unequivocally clear. "But if the case be doubtful, or the rule doubtful, to men of such understanding and parts as your magistrates are," Winthrop insisted, "if your magistrates should err here, yourselves must bear it."

Although Winthrop had prevailed in this instance, his conception of government did not fully suit the people he was attempting to lead. Probably as much from unhappy recollections of arbitrary power at home as from any alternative Puritan doctrine, settlers entering Massachusetts in the 1630s had moved purposefully to decentralize public authority to a degree unknown in the mother country. All legislators and executives were subject to annual election; the governor had virtually no independent role; a major part of colonial governance devolved to the level of the town meeting. The shaky constitutional foundation of these arrangements was a charter organizing a commercial company, which the Puritans had tacitly misinterpreted as a political blueprint for their commonwealth. As early as 1635, too, there was agitation in Massachusetts to frame a body of laws "in resemblence to a Magna Charta." Despite objections by Winthrop, the subsequent statutory compilations of 1641 and 1648 guaranteed many of the traditional "Liberties" of Englishmen—such as trial by jury—that were plainly intended to limit the powers of colonial officialdom. In addition, the Bay colony adopted some decidedly untraditional measures revealing the strength of antiauthoritarian sentiment there. It was stipulated, for example, that "everie man whether Inhabitant or Forreiner, Free or not Free," should have the "libertie to come to any publick Court, Counsell, or town-meeting; and either by his speech or writing, to move any lawfull, seasonable, or material question."

It may be that some New Englanders were consciously trying to devise a political system based on social covenant, by which individuals gathered and consented formally to the rule of law. Since they organized their churches in similar fashion, political covenanting was a process that might have appealed to ordinary settlers as well as ideologues. Many communities in New England came into existence by virtue of collective written promises—the most famous being those recorded in Plymouth's "Mayflower Compact." Such compacts had been conceptualized by political philosophers, but they had never before been put into practice. In 1647, radical Puritans in the mother country were unable to persuade moderate leaders of their revolution to endorse an innovative document that purported to represent the "Agreements of the People." In New England, however, civil covenants were uncontroversial and appear often to have expressed a kind of spontaneous folk feeling for small coherent communities of compatible and participatory citizens. So in 1637, one hundred and twenty-five colonists in Dedham, Massachusetts, signed an agreement by which they pledged "each to other to professe and practice one trueth according to that most perfect rule, The foundation where of is Everlasting Love." Further, they agreed "by all meanes" to prevent the intrusion of "all such" as might be "contrarye minded," and to "become freely subject unto all such orders and constitutions" that might be necessary. Evidently a similar impulse accounted for a compact drawn up a year earlier by eight frontiersmen starting the western Massachusetts town of Springfield. "Wee whose names are underwritten," it began, "beinge by God's p'vidence ingaged to make a Plantation . . . , do mutually agree to certayne articles and orders to be observed and kept by us and our successors, except wee and every of us for ourselves and in our owne p'sons shall thinke meete upon better reasons to alter our p'sent resolution."

This habit of covenanting, along with some other features of New England's early legal system, may also have reflected the shadowy influence of customary law surviving in the English manors and boroughs from which many settlers had emigrated. Just as the founders of a new town might lay out common fields and scatter individual allotments of acreage in an attempt to reproduce the agricultural practices of this or that English village, so they appear to have been guided by memories of ancient local jurisdictions still operative in the mother country outside the range of formalistic royal courts. One settler might recall the constitution of a particular borough; another, a manuscript summary of municipal ordinances kept in the desk of a town clerk. Most had to be at least dimly aware of the elementary procedures followed in those everyday English courts where a husbandman or artisan might find himself if he had left garbage in the streets or wanted to collect a petty bill.

Sustained by some blend of conscious principle and reflexive behavior, then, a distinctively localized pattern of lawmaking emerged in seventeenth-century New England. This was the basis of the

Puritan endeavor to realize shared religious hopes for personal and social reformation. It was the basis, too, of a legal system especially appropriate to small-scale farmers inhabiting tightly knit communities where marked disparities of social and economic position were unusual. In such communities, there was no need to import the bewildering complexities of the common law that to Sir Edward Coke and his learned disciples embodied the "perfection of human reason." Colonial realities meshed with English local tradition and utopian Puritan ideology, allowing New Englanders to benefit from the very program of legal reform that their coreligionists in the mother country sought but failed to implement.

Reformers in England spoke ambitiously of plans to simplify and decentralize the labyrinthine judicial structures of the nation, to reduce "great volumes of law . . . into the bigness of a pocketbook," and to regulate if not abolish the legal profession. All this, presumably, would make justice cheaper and more accessible to the ordinary citizen. Lawyers, among others, blocked most proposals along such lines in the mother country; but in seventeenth-century Massachusetts and other colonies imitating its example, the boldest of legal dreams became fact. There was a unitary court system in the Bible Commonwealth, without the multiplicity of specialized tribunals through which Englishmen had to navigate. Country courts handled the bulk of civil business as well as most routine crimes; they also assumed broad administrative responsibility for everything from the laying out of roads, to settlement of the poor, to maintenance of churches and schools, to regulation of mills, ferries, and other public utilities. At the town level, individual magistrates or resident commissioners for small causes resolved minor civil disputes, performed marriages, tried to suppress drunkenness, and intervened informally in a miscellany of local affairs. Appeals ran to the General Court of the colony, which was also the legislature, or to a Court of Assistants composed of the governor, deputy governor, and magistrates, which also claimed trial jurisdiction over serious crimes and divorce.

From 1648 on, the abundant legal rules of the colony were conveniently packaged in the form of a statutory code alphabetized from A ("Abilities") to W ("Wrecks of the Sea"). With justifiable pride, legislators in Massachusetts pointed out that "in four hundred years" their English counterparts "could not so compile their Lawes." At last it had been done, not coincidentally by a "poor Colonie" that was "unfurnished of Lawyers and Statesmen." This was mock humility, to be sure; but for a time Massachusetts did prohibit anyone from taking a fee to represent someone else in court, and in 1663 it was flatly declared that any "usual and Common Attorney in any Inferior Court" could not sit in the legislature. Not until 1673 was there formal recognition of the right to practice law in the colony, and then fees were strictly regulated. The few men who took up this invitation before the end of the century were poorly trained and lacked enough clients for full-time work. If in need of assistance in managing a case, a litigating colonist could turn to a relative, friend, or business agent.

Predictably, in these circumstances, the mystifying niceties of English legal procedure tended to fall away, leaving just those basics that might be learned by a lay court clerk from a manual such as Michael Dalton's *Countrey Justice* (see Documents, pp. 98–102). The only official language of the courts was English; there was no need to master obscure medieval terminology. Untrained judges joined juries in mixing matters of law with matters of fact. According to statute, a jury that was not "clear" regarding a particular case might choose "in open Court to advise with any man they shall think fit to resolve or direct them, before they give in their verdict." Forms of action were used flexibly. There was little of the technical precision insisted on in the royal courts of the mother country, which pre-scribed rigid verbal formulae for different descriptions of wrongs and requests for remedies. The name of an action that in England would be brought to recover damages for an act of carelessness might be affixed to a colonial lawsuit by a creditor seeking a sum of money or repossession of goods from a debtor. In the absence of highly trained lawyers, there was no one to maintain orthodoxy and no great reason to do so, since simplified procedure was less costly to litigants.

It was natural enough that similar results were reached in other colonies founded by religious idealists. A statute of 1686 in Connecti-cut, for example, made it clear that the courts there should not reverse judgments merely because of mistakes in the form of pleadings. Pennsylvania, perhaps mindful of the "blackness" among lawyers decried long before by the Quaker George Fox, specified in its Judicature Act of 1701 that "Brevity, plainess and verity" were expected in all proceedings. Elsewhere, too, distaste for legal formal-ism and its practitioners was widespread, although the motives involved might be less visionary. One reason lawyers were especially unwelcome in late-seventeenth-century New York may have been the opportunity they had there to exploit Anglo-Dutch antagonisms. In Virginia, from the outset, turbulent local figures expressed contempt for "men of law" representing the interests of a distant commercial company. Later in the century, planters fearful of executive patronage power repeatedly frustrated initiatives by the governor to professionalize legal practice in the colony by a system of licensing. There were also the usual mutterings that lawyers stirred up and prolonged expensive litigation, to the "great prejudice of the people." Hence a statute of 1658 urging courts in Virginia to render judgment "according as the right of the cause and the matter in lawe shall appeare unto them, without regard of any imperfection, default or want of forme in any writt, returne, plaint or proces." This was language to which Puritans would not have objected.

Despite superficial similarities, however, the legal environment of both Virginia and Maryland in the seventeenth century differed significantly from that of New England. Early Chesapeake society had not formed around compact agricultural communities. Because settlement there was dispersed, as a consequence of runaway tobacco production, judicial and administrative authority barely existed below the county level and was disturbingly attenuated where its presence could be felt (see Documents, pp. 102–105). Indeed, it was the peculiar logistics of the region that made formality in law seem particularly undesirable to some people. Distances were such that a litigant might be greatly inconvenienced if he took a case to court, having assembled witnesses for the occasion, only to have to turn around and go back home because of an error in procedure. Since a county grandee might be able to take advantage of such a situation, this was a problem that in some instances could aggravate divisions within a society marked by distinct gradations of rank and wealth.

As administrative units, county courts in the Chesapeake colonies claimed much the same authority to regulate economic affairs as was exercised at both the town and the county level in New England. Effective enforcement was another matter, in a region without nucleated settlements or strong communal habits of decision making. Nothing would have better promoted the general welfare of Maryland and Virginia in their early years than strict curtailment of tobacco production to keep up prices. It was both a symptom and a cause of social fragility there that legislative measures to this effect failed miserably. Planters with vast stretches of land, often the very county officials expected to implement the law, simply went their own way and cultivated more acreage. Toward the end of the century, in a series of explosive "plant-cutting" riots, small-scale farmers attempted unsuccessfully to improve conditions by extralegal action. Regulation of the tobacco trade did not become feasible for another several decades, when leading planters finally recognized that it was in their mutual interest to establish a system of public warehouses for inspection of quality and packing practices. The story of tobacco was the story of the region. Public authority rested on shallow social foundations.

Like the Church of England in Virginia, legal institutions in the Chesapeake colonies could give an impression of ritualized formality that belied the facts. In spite of criticism, judges in both Maryland and Virginia tended to be more willing than those in New England to consider and sustain arguments on narrow technical grounds, but their overall performance was inconsistent and arbitrary. In 1666, for example, a case involving a capital charge of grand larceny came before the Provincial Court of Maryland. Sympathetic jurors adopted a stratagem time-tested in English courtrooms and tried to spare the defendant by undervaluing the property stolen, a cow, in order to reclassify the crime as a lesser offense. Told by the court to deliberate again and "have a special care in what they did," they withdrew their finding. The court then pronounced the death sentence, whereupon "friends" of the condemned man rose to beg for mercy and thus obtained a respite. The respite remained in force for a full decade and was followed by a pardon. Whether or not rough justice had been done, judicial behavior here was quite unpredictable by rules of law.

Local proceedings in the mother country, to the distress of the king's judges on circuit, were sometimes no more orderly than what went on in seventeenth-century Chesapeake courts. Remote from royal influence, however, the authorities in Maryland and Virginia found it particularly difficult to create an atmosphere of respect for the legal process. Traces of ceremony here and there seemed oddly out of place. Judges of Maryland's Provincial Court were expected to appear wearing their official ribbons and medals. One county attorney in Virginia was said to own two silk gowns, although he had no prospect of using them, and carried his papers ostentatiously in an English barrister's bag. Yet in general, Chesapeake justice had a frontier look rowdier than what was usual in the mother country—and rarely to be found in New England. Judges in oversized counties were notoriously reluctant to leave the comforts of home and travel in bad weather; chronic absenteeism was a feature of many courts. Until late in the century, when most counties constructed modest courthouses, judicial proceedings were often held in taverns, where all concerned were likely to grow abusive. Criminals might be lodged in the same place as well, for lack of prison facilities. A sheriff in Maryland once complained that he had no jail in the vicinity "but his own hands." In Virginia, a man accused of escaping from detention pleaded drunkenness as his excuse.

But it was not only the forms of early American law that differed according to local social circumstances. Substance varied too. This might be so even where the wording of specific provisions appeared uniform from one colonial jurisdiction to another. In practice, similar laws could take on divergent social meanings, informed by the special conditions to which they were supposed to apply.

Statutes in New England, for example, accorded with one in Virginia requiring every landowner to "enclose his ground with sufficient fences or else to plant, uppon their owne perill." What this indicated was that an owner of horses or cattle would not be liable for damage they might cause in a neighbor's field if the neighbor had failed to make a reasonable effort to guard against such a possibility. Here the colonies deviated from English law, which held the owner of animals liable whether or not the neighbor's land was fenced. Everywhere, it may be speculated, the colonial rule reflected the importance of encouraging settlers to import and breed livestock, and perhaps too the relative availability of timber. But other factors were in play as well. In the average town of early New England, where differences in wealth were apt to be inconsiderable and cattle might be distributed approximately in proportion to acreage, the costs of such a public policy were shared more or less equitably by most inhabitants. In Virginia, however, fencing laws provoked deep social hostility. Whether or not they fully enclosed their fields, large-scale planters were far less vulnerable to devastation caused by mischievous animals than were subsistence farmers cultivating small plots. Moreover, it was the large-scale planters who kept the animals that made the worst trouble. The problem finally bubbled to the top in 1670, when a statute was passed ordering owners of unruly horses to take care to control them during the corn season—"it being much fitter that rich men who have the benefitt of such horses should provide for their restraint, than the poor enjoyned to the impossibility of . . . high fences." The very next year, in Maryland, the

Assembly confronted the same issue from another angle by trying to prohibit further importation of horses into the colony, on the grounds that they were "destructive to the inhabitants." Good fences might help to make good neighbors in New England; in the Chesapeake region, where neighborliness was lacking to begin with, fencing policy only aggravated tensions.

In some respects, seventeenth-century Chesapeake conditions resembled those of a poor rural area in England. Probably no category of behavior occupied the Maryland authorities to a greater extent than hog stealing. Elaborate efforts were made to record the markings on stock; punishments prescribed by statute included branding on the shoulder with an "H" for a second offense and death for a third. More generally, both Maryland and Virginia retained much of England's harsh criminal law protecting small as well as large amounts of property. As in the mother country, pardons and commutations softened its application, sometimes only after a bizarre ritual in which the condemned man would not be told of his reprieve until the rope was put about his neck. One early example of reform legislation, passed by the Maryland Assembly in 1681, aimed systematically to alleviate the "severity of the Laws of England against all thieving, stealing and purloining." Its rationale revealed not stability but disarray in Chesapeake society. All capital offenses had to be tried in the Provincial Court at St. Mary's, and this of course was inconvenient in a colony "so meanly and thinly inhabited." It was expedient, therefore, to reduce the penalties for minor thefts and let such crimes be disposed of at the county level. Such a solution neither reflected nor prompted local confidence in the security of property.

To the north, by contrast, both the Puritans and the Quakers chose from the beginning to rely much less on the threat of execution to prevent crimes against property, although within a few decades Pennsylvania started to revert to the grim deterrent policy of the mother country. Massachusetts, in 1642, deferred capital punishment for robbery or burglary—far more alarming crimes than simple theft—until a third conviction, whereas in England this was the prescribed sentence for a first offender. In many cases of minor theft that were capital crimes by English law, the usual Puritan penalty was a whipping and double or triple restitution to the victim. In all, despite their more rigorous Hebraic classification of some moral offenses, New Englanders altered English law to decrease the number of capital crimes, at a time when that number was increasing in the mother country. Specifically, too, Massachusetts prohibited punishments considered "In-humane, barbarous or cruel."

Idealism surely figured here; but this was also a model of penal legislation that made pragmatic sense in a society largely free of unsettling conflict between the very rich and the very poor. It made sense in a society composed mainly of small landowners enjoying security of title. Outside New England most acreage was, at least in theory, subject to demands for annual rent by the Crown or by a proprietor. Little as this was likely to matter in practice, it was the pride of seventeenth-century Puritan colonists that their original charters had established a system of widespread landholding without even symbolic feudal features. If their laws had one overriding purpose, it was to maintain that system indefinitely, as the basis of cohesive communal life.

This was the reason that New Englanders from the early years of settlement wanted all transfers of houses and acreage to be publicly recorded, and insisted that the public record of every transfer—in the form of a deed registered according to standard regulations—normally guaranteed title, although another person might produce unregistered evidence of a prior claim to the same property. Formal registration, it was explained by the General Court of Massachusetts, would offer "sufficient assurance" of everyone's legal rights. There were local English models for such a procedure; but it represented a significant improvement on practices in the mother country for many settlers, who as tenant farmers faced with eviction had experienced difficulty in manorial courts when they tried to justify their claims by means of oral testimony. Although most colonies south of New England made similar arrangements to record land titles, there was seldom the same sense of urgent public interest in the process. Maryland, for its part, declined to recognize the priority of a registered deed over other titles. Nor do other colonists seem to have been as intent as New Englanders on conducting private litigation to clarify any remaining doubts as to the validity and extent of their titles. Before the middle of the seventeenth century, when there was more than enough land in eastern Massachusetts to go around, elements of uncertainty here and there might be overlooked—if nothing of great value were at stake. Afterward, as the older Puritan towns grew crowded, their residents turned to the county courts for judgments that would resolve definitively who owned what. Often these actions were collusive; sometimes a sharp, aggressive individual would attempt to exploit the formalities of the system (see Documents, pp. 105–108). Clergymen, toward the end of the century, began to lament the rising tendency of New Englanders to sue one another, in violation of brotherly Christian ethics, but most people in the region were more concerned to regularize their affairs as landholders.

If the utopian aspirations of the first generation in New England faded rather quickly, except in discourse from the pulpit, their commitment to a well-ordered and diffusely prosperous society continued to be influential. The original compact of a town such as Dedham could not be replicated from decade to decade, but New Englanders were adaptive and learned to organize their social life on somewhat different terms. Dreams of brotherhood proved unrealistic, as some towns were torn apart by prolonged disputes that threatened to eventuate in mob violence—"club law," as it was called. In such cases, the practical solution was to allow the dissidents to found a new town of their own. Since it was in the interest of every citizen to be able to dispose of his property freely at market value, few communities persisted in refusing to let individual inhabitants sell land to outsiders or in requiring that people who moved away without permission forfeit their local titles.

To keep their towns intact and peaceful, seventeenth-century New Englanders relied less on coercive legal measures than on incentives and restraints resulting from the effective family organization of property rights. Law helped here, but usually not by interfering with the freedom of particular landholders to make transactions as they pleased. With land abundant, New England differed from the mother country in having few estates that were "entailed" so as to restrict the right of descendants to sell off family acreage; those few were open to legal challenge and easily undone. It was simply expected that each succeeding generation of parents would arrange to divide up land and other property by terms that adequately served all children and encouraged them to settle in the same locality.

Family, the "little commonwealth" that formed the core of the larger polity, was the most important mechanism of successful communal life in early New England. Appropriately, its legal framework was less authoritarian than the model recognized in the mother country. However traditionally Puritans might enjoin a wife to be "Obedient and Subject to her Husband" by the "Law of God," however conspicuously they upheld the customary double standard in their disinclination to prosecute a married man for adultery with a single woman, they tended to deviate from one-sided English law in their regulation of relationships between the sexes. In addition to annulments on account of impotence or bigamy, which had been available in the ecclesiastical courts of the mother country, women in early New England could obtain civil divorces for such reasons as desertion or cruelty, although only in Connecticut did this ever become anything more than a rare option requiring exceptional tenacity and resourcefulness. Perhaps in part because women in seventeenth-century New England were actually responsible for key managerial functions within the domestic economy, it seems that they gained at least some status within the local legal system. In 1650, Massachusetts made it a crime for either spouse to strike the other. In the colony of Plymouth, it was as likely for a man to be punished because he abused his wife by "kiking her of from a stoole into the fier" as for a woman accused of "beating and reviling her husband, and egging her children to healp her, bidding them knock him in the head, and wishing his victuals might coak him." A court might well void a husband's "irrational and unrighteous Will" if it left a "frugall and laborious" widow with an inadequate share of his estate. Her rights to a portion of that estate, in any case, were apt to be defined more broadly than in the mother country.

The very simplification of justice in early New England made it easier in practice for married women there to assert some limited legal personality, instead of having their decision-making powers submerged under those of their husbands according to the formulae of the royal courts at Westminister. Without any need of enforcing such an arrangement by special recourse to a chancery court, a Massachusetts woman might contract before marriage for the free-dom afterward to dispose of specified property "att her owne free will from time to time, and att any time," regardless of her husband's wishes. Postnuptial contracts were much less common, but a married woman would not expect legal complications if separately identified in her father's will as the recipient of one bequest while her husband was named for another. Informally, too, many married women were able to conduct legal business of their own and on behalf of or jointly with their husbands.

As for the relationship of parents to children, New England's policy was overtly untraditional. Hebraic disciplinary laws were on the books, but intergenerational family affairs normally seem to have been managed in such a way as to emphasize mutuality of interest. Outside Rhode Island, where legal institutions adhered to the example of the mother country, New Englanders indicated how they conceptualized the "little commonwealth" by abandoning the English rule known as primogeniture, according to which the eldest son succeeded to the entire estate of a man who died without making a will. Instead, all children but the eldest male got equal portions—an arrangement that may have been influenced by localized custom in some counties of the mother country; by Mosaic precept, the first son received a double share.

Although there was some disagreement from the start regarding the origins and legal justification of this formula, which was not codified until late in the seventeenth century, its social utility was always obvious enough. It was a way to maintain that "equallitie which is the rule of God," in a country where, unlike Old England, "Mankind are more wanted than land to subdue & Cultivate ye Earth and Defend its Inhabitants." It was a way of rewarding younger children, "generally having been longest and most serviceable unto their parents," and of making it unnecessary for them to "rove about the world for bread." Not surprisingly, then, it was a rule that New Englanders—an unusually literate people for their time—tended to observe voluntarily when they took the common precaution of drawing up wills. And it was a rule that often governed the process by which, during their frequently long lifetimes, they might gradually turn over property to their children. The net effect of such provisions within a particular family could indeed favor not only the eldest male but the youngest child too, since it was he or she who most probably would have to care for the surviving parent or parents in old age.

This pattern of inheritance in early New England met the larger needs of the local community especially well because most families appear to have negotiated property rights among themselves and thus effectively resolved potential conflicts. Some fathers might retain title to all their lands even after their children had come of age and married, but there was a threat of last resort if this proved truly disagreeable. So in Plymouth, a younger son named Joseph Ryder warned that he would "Goe away" unless his father marked off a plot on which he could build a house and not be "Molested." If Joseph went, his mother said, she would "Goe" too. The father yielded, grudgingly, and another generation was staked to the community.

Pennsylvania followed New England's rules in its general laws of inheritance; New York, Maryland, Virginia, and the Carolinas retained the English doctrine singling out the eldest son in the · absence of a will and, at least on paper, were less permissive in undoing the restrictions of "entailed" estates. Everywhere south of New England, women benefited to some degree in the early stages of settlement from informality of legal procedure, although divorce was unobtainable even on the limited scale of the Puritan colonies. In the Chesapeake region throughout the seventeenth century, however, neither carryovers nor deviations from the law of the mother country were of lasting consequence, for the basic reason that the family unit of parents and children could not function there as a central stabilizing institution within local society.

Optimistically, Chesapeake planters might say that their extended world of friends and servants and slaves constituted a large familial order, but they rarely reversed the direction of the metaphor to claim—as New Englanders did—that the family was a miniature state. Indeed, they had little cause to do so, since family life in the early Chesapeake colonies often crossed the borderlines of pathology. For much of the seventeenth century, women were scarce and the life expectancy of males dismally low. Not only did these conditions contribute to the fervent language of various laws against miscegenation; they prompted Chesapeake legislators to devise orphans' courts with elaborate supervisory powers. Recognized here was the serious possibility that the estate or labor of a child might be exploited by "many stepfathers" and an "unkareful mother," particularly if there was no local network of kinfolk to watch over them. Another curious legal feature of the region, symptomatic of fragile family life, was the practice by which a husband and a wife would contract for the better management not of their property but of themselves. "Frances shall henceforth forbear to call him ye sd John any vile names or give him any ill language," read one such agreement in early eighteenth-century Virginia. Other postnuptial contracts, implying impressive practical additions to the legal personality of married women, acknowledged de facto separations according to terms that would have been impermissible in New England.

As time went on and mortality rates became less severe, Chesapeake planters developed a legal framework for regulation of family affairs that typically mixed Old World forms and distinctive regional habits. Like New Englanders, eighteenth-century Virginians seldom "entailed" their estates, and it was possible with some ingenuity to circumvent the rules applying to those few that were thus restricted. The great majority of planters who drew up wills made provision for younger children, although the eldest son normally inherited the home plantation (see Documents, pp. 108–112). Younger sons might receive outlying or western lands previously worked by tenants, or cash settlements might be arranged—perhaps for daughters as well. One indication that family life in the region continued to be diffuse was the common practice of making secondary bequests to siblings, cousins, nephews, and unrelated friends. Widows were usually assured of an adequate share, until remarriage if not for their lifetimes; but the tendency was to appoint others to manage the family property. The prospects of widowhood were improved somewhat because slaves counted as real estate for the purpose of inheritance; unlike land, they were a movable kind of property that allowed owners extra flexibility in adjusting resources to meet changing economic needs.

Regarding the numerous wards that a Chesapeake planter might oversee working his fields, servants as well as slaves, the laws of the region could be vicious. Whereas in New England a servant "in want of competent and convenient clothing" might successfully bring a complaint in court, if he or she lacked nearby relatives who were prepared to help, it often required evidence of outrageous brutality to persuade a county court in Maryland or Virginia to intervene. The saga of Captain Thomas Bradnox, a choleric drunkard who was a justice of the peace and former sheriff of Kent County in seventeenth-century Maryland, revealed the very worst tendencies of an oppressive legal system. Bradnox regularly beat a young female servant until she ran away; apprehended and returned, she was beaten again. In the end she was able to persuade the county court to release her from her indenture only when it was established that Bradnox, who could not even sign his name, had smashed a stool over her head because he came upon her reading a book. On appeal, it was determined that the county court would have to compensate Bradnox for his loss of her service. This same master was responsible for the death of another servant, a young man who had been beaten and then imprisoned for six days without food and water. Mrs. Bradnox was evidently capable of similar brutality, particularly toward any servant who chanced to witness her in an act of infidelity.

Chesapeake law usually did little to restrain an intemperate master or mistress. What it did do was to whip runaways and extend their terms of service, by a rate of as many as ten days for every one in absence. Female servants bearing children—"to the great dishonour of God, and the apparent damage to the masters, or owners, of such servants"—might have to serve extra time. Early in the eighteenth century, North Carolina set the additional term for such an offense at two full years, unless the master himself was identified as the father. The flagrant partiality of the legal system, insofar as it was concerned with white servitude, was well exemplified by the decision of one coroner's jury in Maryland to indict a servant girl for "self-murder"; she had gone off and drowned herself after a savage beating from her mistress.

Of course black slaves fared even worse in the colonial system of justice. A master could expect to be immune from prosecution if his slave died as a result of "moderate" correction. One fatal example of such correction, which turned out to be unindictable, involved a slaveowner in seventeenth-century Maryland who had beaten a black man named Antonio, poured hot lard over his back, and then hung him by the hands half-naked in a cold wind. The logic of tender legal treatment for a master who had killed his slave was made unpleasantly clear early on in Virginia. It could not be "presumed," according to a statute of 1669, "that prepensed malice (which alone makes murther Felony) should induce any man to destroy his own estate." Implicit here was a massive irony in the legal system of slavery. Masters, motivated by self-interest, could not always be trusted to enforce the laws vigorously against people whom they owned, lest the value of their investment be diminished. Unlike white servants, slaves could not be threatened with longer terms, and there were obvious reasons for wanting to avoid having them executed. The harsh capital laws applying to slaves who committed felonies had to be mitigated in practice, although the quality of mercy involved was quite different from what prompted the usual maneuvers to spare white criminals. Perhaps the greatest danger of all lay outside the courtroom. Several jurisdictions in the eighteenth century promised public compensation not only to owners of slaves who were executed but also to owners of those who died during capture. The sum of money fixed by law might not be the equivalent, however, of replacing a trained hand. If a slave escaped, all whites in the area would be unleashed in his pursuit, with license to kill. In such a situation, which lawfully invited poor citizens to destroy the property of their social superiors, the deepest contradictions within white society might become luridly apparent.

This could happen in a northern port town as well as in a rural southern county. New York City, in the spring of 1741, was swept by rumors of a vast conspiracy among its slaves, who probably accounted for more than 15 percent of the population. A series of suspicious fires fueled anxiety. Coached by the authorities, a young white woman who worked as a servant for a local tavern keeper supplied details of what the attorney general pronounced to be the "most horrible and destructive plot that ever was yet known in these northern parts of America." Supposedly, blacks planned to burn the town down and install as "King" the very tavern keeper who employed this key informant. Accusations mushroomed. By the time the law had done its job, four whites and eighteen blacks had been hanged; thirteen more blacks had been burned to death and another seventy deported. Besides the tavern keeper, one of the white victims was a nomadic dancemaster said to be a "popish priest" in disguise. As the prosecution explained, black slaves were merely "inferior and subordinate agents" in an intricate scheme that "took its rise from a foreign influence." Once it was understood that a minion of the Roman Catholic church was in their midst, the "secret springs" of the entire dark drama were unveiled.

Fittingly, one official received an anonymous letter comparing such fantastic speculation to the hysteria of the "Bloody Tragedy" that had occurred a half century earlier at Salem. More than a small circle of suspected witches was involved. Blacks were everywhere, as white New Yorkers were well aware—"these enemies of their own household." If some leading citizens dared to suggest that "there was no plot at all," no one could deny the reality of the fires. A few people recognized them for what they almost certainly were, diversionary tactics to cover looting by a ring of blacks, white prostitutes, and other unsavory figures from the local underworld. As in Salem, the net of accusations widened to include the names of prominent "people *in ruffles*." The hard truth, in mid-eighteenth-century New York, was that such men owned slaves and so indeed had a substantial stake in stopping the prosecutions, which jeopardized their property.

Urban colonial society was growing turbulent and tense. Although blacks in New York proved controllable after 1741, executions of white criminals increased noticeably in the next few decades.

Throughout the colonies, legislators generally saw no urgent reason to expand the range of capital offenses to the terrifying degree considered necessary by their counterparts in eighteenth-century England. Indeed, there was rising concern in some jurisdictions—Virginia, for example—to regularize the various informal mechanisms by which death sentences were apt to be avoided. Here and there in colonial America, however, circumstances were such as to emphasize the role of the executioner as a guardian of the social order. South Carolina, at the beginning of the revolutionary era, had ten times as many capital crimes listed in its legal code as did Massachusetts.

Even in New England, by the middle of the eighteenth century, communal life was disconcertingly less resilient than before. Regulation of prices and wages was a practice of the past. Boston long before had come to be regarded by the pious as a kind of regional Babylon, teeming with unattached people and harbor vice. Such people had started to take to the roads, moving from town to town in search of work; at each stop, lest their poverty impose a burden on local taxpayers, they were likely to be "warned out" of the vicinity. Meanwhile, the native population of the older New England towns had swelled to the point where frequently just one son in a family would inherit the entire homestead. The others, in a pattern that somewhat resembled the more generous arrangements made by affluent Chesapeake planters, might emigrate to frontier land or hope to be established in trades. Widows found it ever more difficult to subsist on property subject to competing claims by different children. Fierce arguments raged in some towns over individual rights to land originally designated as common pasture and woodlots. Indebtedness was widespread. Although debtors were better off than in the mother country, where imprisonment was a constant possibility, some New Englanders worried publicly that freehold farmers would one day "become Tenants to the Lenders, and pay Rent to them." Then, in a little time, there would be no "middling Sort" left in local society, but instead "a very few Lords, and all the rest Beggars." Old communal ways still persisted in many parts of the region, but the future seemed uncertain.

Yet the traditions of the previous century remained vital, outside New England as well as within. Nowhere was the force of communal habit felt more powerfully, in the decades before the Revolution, than on the great manorial estates that lay along the Hudson River in New York. These huge tracts of land, assembled amid the factional maneuverings of elite politicians in the colony, were cultivated by tenants according to the terms of leases varying in length from a specified number of years to perpetuity. Rents were modest, but the small farmers of the area—many of whom had moved there from New England—had other grievances. To transfer a lease, a tenant might have to pay his landlord a fee equal to as much as one-fourth the market value of his farm. He might have to take his grain to a proprietary mill and pay whatever price was asked there. If mistreated, he had reason to doubt that local officialdom would be independent enough to give him a fair hearing. These were conditions that some colonists might have tolerated, but not former New Englanders accustomed to a different model of social organization. In the 1750s, they brawled repeatedly with proprietary representatives along the Hudson. Then, in 1765, the heirs to the Philipse Highland Patent in Dutchess County began to evict settlers near the Connecticut border, whose titles derived from recently invalidated Indian claims. Soon the entire region was in turmoil, as companies of armed farmers roamed the countryside in protest. It was not until royal troops appeared on the scene that the rebellion dissipated; one of its leaders was sentenced to death, but he was subsequently pardoned by George III.

The spectacle of colonial farmers rioting on behalf of secure title was ominous, coming as it did in the middle of the Stamp Act crisis. These were not lawless people by habit. Colonial conditions had seldom given them occasion to sustain the traditional forms of crowd violence and dissent that were so familiar in the mother country. But their behavior suggested that in some circumstances, where norms of communal welfare were violated, recourse to higher law would appear quite appropriate. Some two decades earlier, in defense of land rioters in New Jersey, it had been argued that their very "Numbers, Violences, and unlawful Action" demonstrated how "wronged & oppressed" they were—"or else they would never *rebell agt. the Laws.*" Local consensus was a law unto itself, perhaps superior in legitimacy to injurious external authority. In 1768, some such reasoning prompted even Thomas Hutchinson, Massachusetts's most prominent Tory, to concede that "Mobs, a sort of them at least, are constitutional."

FOUR

The Stresses of Empire

Overlaying the localized development of early American law and society, from the late seventeenth century onward, was an expanding program of imperial administration that gradually left its mark on both institutions and political leadership in the mainland colonies. The major public consequences of increased English intervention in colonial affairs have been described often and well, but some features of the new system deserve particular consideration here because of their effect on previously established patterns of American legal experience. That experience, so modified, would influence the role of law and lawyers in the debates and events of the Revolution.

English supervision of colonial America did not begin in earnest until 1675, when the Committee of the Privy Council on Trade and Plantations was formed. For more than a decade, with a rigor that had not been seen before and was never duplicated afterward, this administrative body pursued a policy of colonial centralization under royal auspices. The vagaries of English political life, along with the disruptions of the Glorious Revolution in 1688–1689, soon undid much of its work. In 1696, it was succeeded by a Board of Trade with broad responsibility to assemble information about the colonies but no formal power to govern them. It proposed legislation to Parliament and recommended disallowance of colonial statutes to the Privy Council.

Other English agencies were involved in the management of the empire overseas. The secretary of state for the Southern Department selected royal governors, often but not always on the advice of the

Board of Trade; the commissioners of Customs, a bureau within the Treasury Board, were expected to enforce the commercial regulations embodied in the various Navigation Acts passed during the second half of the seventeenth century; the Admiralty, or Navy Department, assisted customs collectors and tried to suppress piracy; the War Office had charge of military planning. These and other administrative units, including the office of the bishop of London, competed for position in the governance of the colonies. Each normally had a say, for the sake of private patronage as well as public policy, in writing up official instructions that the Board of Trade transmitted to royal governors. They were the chief representatives of the Crown in most colonies, although not in the self-governing chartered enclaves of Connecticut and Rhode Island, nor in the surviving proprietary jurisdictions of Pennsylvania and Maryland. In any case, they had little effective control over most other royal appointees sent out to America, and their sweeping formal authority to curtail the deliberations of provincial assemblies and veto legislation in the name of the Crown was illusory. Without substantial patronage at their disposal, and sensitive to crosscurrents of pressure from the mother country, they were seldom able to master the turbulently factional games of colonial politics. English policy reached eighteenth-century America in bits and pieces, rarely in coherent and compelling form.

Inevitably, as regulation of the colonies proliferated, conflicts with imperial officialdom became more frequent and acute. Only once before the revolutionary era, however, was there a confrontation focused enough to prompt colonists to pose radical questions concerning the constitution of the empire. This happened early, under the activist Privy Council committee established in 1675, and took shape most dramatically in Massachusetts after its charter had been vacated in 1684 and it was incorporated into an extensive but short-lived new jurisdiction called the Dominion of New England. Late in 1686, Governor Edmund Andros arrived in Boston harbor, empowered by James II to pass laws and raise taxes for the dominion merely with the consent of an appointive council. His "detested" reign, aborted at the time of the Glorious Revolution in the mother country, was a nightmarish political episode that touched the raw nerves of New Englanders and would be remembered by them on the eve of independence for the "heart-felt animosity" it had aroused.

Andros taunted orthodox Puritans mercilessly, celebrating Christmas with "popish" ostentation and even permitting construction of a maypole in Charlestown. English forms and customs were introduced into local judicial proceedings, including the flagrantly un-Puritan requirement that a witness had to take an oath by kissing the Bible instead of simply putting one hand on it and raising the other. A new superior court system aroused fear at the county level of interference by itinerant judges from outside. Andros also threatened to undermine the security of land titles in the region. Many of the grants made by Massachusetts, on the basis of its original charter from Charles I, were technically defective. Some, to individuals, lacked a proper seal. Others, made to towns, were invalid anyway because by English law the town meetings of the colony were not corporate legal entities authorized to hold or grant land. A corporation, which was what the chartered Bay colony had been, could not create another corporation; therefore, in theory, most of the land being farmed in Andros's dominion had to revert to its ultimate overlord—the king. Although Andros was willing to accept far less than that, he insisted on fees for confirmation of questionable titles, attempted to assess uniform feudal rents on reissued patents as well as on new grants of vacant lands, and encouraged his political allies to petition for large tracts of undivided common acreage that town meetings could no longer claim to own. New Englanders had to admit that they had not strictly observed "the formality of the Law"; but surely their "title to the . . . rights of *Englishmen*" should protect them against such tyrannical measures. "Besides . . .," argued one pamphleteer after Andros's dominion had collapsed, "there was *an original contract* between the king and the first planters in *New-England*, the king promising them, if they at their own cost and charge would subdue a wilderness . . ., they and their posterity after them should enjoy such privileges as are in their charters expressed." One such privilege, significant long afterward, was "that of not having taxes imposed on them without their own consent." Not only was this a traditional English "liberty"; it was additionally guaranteed by solemn royal covenant. Plainly, Andros's actions had been "contrary to the laws of God and men."

There would be no further struggle of such magnitude for three-quarters of a century; but localized popular opposition to English officialdom flared up from time to time. Probably no English policy provoked greater grassroots hostility in the colonies than impressment. In 1747, for example, Commodore Charles Knowles triggered a two-day riot when he tried to sweep the Boston waterfront for able-bodied seamen. Whatever the military necessities, this was perceived as an injury to the public welfare because it drained labor from the docks and thus slowed down commerce in the vicinity. Even from the English point of view, press gangs operated on the borderline of legality. Typically, given the administrative muddle of the empire, it was unclear to all concerned whether a naval officer had to request and receive the formal consent of a royal governor and his council before entering a particular jurisdiction to make off with some of its inhabitants.

Enforcement of the White Pine Acts was another source of intermittent friction with the colonial populace. These measures, passed by Parliament in 1722 and 1729, reserved for naval use by the Crown trees that were the principal forest growth in many New England communities. Statutory exemptions were supposed to protect the timberland of towns and private individuals, but an overzealous surveyor might well stretch his instructions in such a way as to challenge the "general interest of the country." Was it justifiable to seize boards processed from illegally felled trees? In 1734 the people of Exeter, New Hampshire, who knew an injustice when they saw one, insisted that such a seizure was unauthorized and rioted in protest against an arbitrary imperial invasion of their rights. Similarly, energetic customs inspectors who confiscated goods according to the letter of the law—or sometimes not—could stir up violent local passions. To an inflamed colonial imagination shaped by folk memories of Old World corruption, they resembled the hated excisemen of the mother country, reputed to be extortionists who took malicious pleasure in physically intimidating helpless victims. In accordance with English traditions of popular political morality, rioting against such official criminality was understood to be a lawful exercise in self-defense.

Mostly, however, the impact of eighteenth-century English governance was less visibly unsettling to colonial society. Miscellaneous parliamentary acts that applied expressly to the colonies were inconvenient or harmful to some merchants and to others hoping to prosper within a commercial empire regulated for the benefit of the mother country. In support of English mercantilist policy, the Privy Council disallowed somewhat more than 5 percent of colonial statutory law. Yet there were few political leaders in America inclined to dispute openly the theoretical groundwork of imperial authority before the 1760s, when Parliament adopted such innovative revenue measures as the Stamp Act and the Townshend Duties. Until then, transatlantic constitutional issues were apt to assume subtler forms. To the extent that discussion focused on colonial legal institutions, the most sensitive point of controversy was the structure of the judiciary.

English goals were relatively consistent in this respect, although implementation was often piecemeal. Edmund Andros's encroachment on the county court system of Massachusetts was part of a long-range trend. Colonial courts were to be reorganized, as far as possible, in conformity with the centralized model of royal justice in the mother country. Efforts along these lines in New York had dated almost from the beginning of English rule there, when governor Richard Nicolls moved to enhance the jurisdiction of appointive justices of the peace at the expense of constables and overseers elected at the town level. In 1691, following the turmoil of Leisler's Rebellion, an Act for Establishing Courts of Judicature brought to completion the cautious reforms of previous decades in New York by consolidating local justice within a county court system and setting that system under the authority of a Supreme Court of Judicature that combined the functions of the royal courts at Westminster. In cases involving more than £100, appeals were allowed to the governor and Council; where more than £300 was at stake, it was possible to proceed to the Privy Council in England. Elsewhere, around and after the turn of the century, the drift of policy was much the same, although provincial legislators were sometimes balky. In 1707, for example, the Maryland Assembly simply refused to finance a new layer of centralized judicial personnel that the royal governor of the colony had tried to introduce at the request of the Board of Trade.

Meanwhile, heeding the recommendations of the same administrative agency, the Privy Council made clear that it would disallow colonial statutes designed to keep control of legal decision making in local hands. Starting with an act of 1701, subsequently struck down in the mother country, a group of Pennsylvania politicians led by David Lloyd battled unsuccessfully for some twenty years to define broad jurisdiction for the county courts of their colony and to limit sharply the authority of its Supreme or Provincial Court. For its part, the Privy Council was concerned to inhibit the power of tribunals that—as an influential English administrator later explained—dispensed "Summary and Domestick Justice" resulting in "much petty Tyranny." What seemed arbitrary from the perspective of the mother country, however, might look quite different in the colonies. In 1735, when the Privy Council disallowed a New Hampshire act removing inferior courts from Portsmouth to inland timbering towns, no one could fail to appreciate that imperial supervision of colonial judicial systems would strengthen the hand of imperial officials charged with enforcing unpopular parliamentary legislation. Such supervision would also help to protect the private interests of English merchants who extended credit to the colonies.

Ultimately, according to the centralized model of judicial authority that English administrators favored, the Privy Council itself was to function as the supreme appellate court of the empire. This was not altogether to the liking of some colonists. In 1710, for example, the General Assembly of Connecticut declared its opinion that "they" could not "oblige any of her Majesties subjects to answer appeals before her Majesty in Council." Massachusetts, ever alert to imperial intrusion, was slyly obstructive. At most Privy Council hearings it was impermissible to introduce evidence not already incorporated in colonial court records. By deliberately attenuating those records so that they lacked essential information, provincial court clerks could easily impede the appellate process.

That process, in any event, was inefficient and confusing. Requirements as to who could appeal in what circumstances varied from colony to colony, and the expense of appealing could be prohibitive. It cost one Rhode Island clergyman more than £350 to seek a final determination of what the term "orthodox minister" meant within the context of a local grant. For all that, the ruling he obtained was inconclusive. Deliberations of the Privy Council were usually prolonged and haphazard. Councilors came and went, many with little or no legal training; most were preoccupied with domestic English politics. Their acquaintance with colonial affairs was likely to be minimal. It was difficult to know in advance what they would do—or afterward what they had in fact done, since their main instrument of decision was an oral order that was rarely printed or even circulated in manuscript. Sometimes they might appear attached to "very narrow principles of mode and form," but on other occasions they took account of "large ideas of right and policy." It was natural, then, that few colonists valued this appellate forum. More cases went to the Privy Council from Rhode Island than from any other mainland colony, but the rate of appeal there was still only about one per year.

Overall, the judicial impact of the Privy Council on colonial legal institutions was simply to increase uncertainty. "No one can tell what is law and what is not in the plantations," observed "An American" at the beginning of the eighteenth century. The Privy Council did little to clarify matters, and was capable of making things worse. Usually it seemed willing to countenance reasonable colonial deviations from English law as long as there was no conflict with the purposes of parliamentary statutes that specifically named the colonies. From time to time, however, this policy lapsed. Most distressing, perhaps, was a case from Connecticut called *Winthrop v. Lechmere*, which culminated in an order of 1728 annulling a major provision of inheritance law in that colony—the traditional Puritan division of an estate, where there was no will, among all children (see Documents, pp. 112–116). Characteristically, the Privy Council failed to follow through here. It subsequently gave approval to a similar Massachusetts law and let Connecticut continue in its former ways without ever saying unequivocally that it could do so. Such erratic judicial behavior led some colonists and English administrators alike, by the 1760s, to toy with proposals for the construction of a special appellate court that would serve the continental colonies.

By orthodox English doctrine, the "power of erecting Courts of Judicature" was "the unalterable prerogative of the Crown." If that prerogative power was too distant when exercised from London, it was far too immediate when institutionalized under the auspices of royal governors representing the king. These beleaguered officials claimed expansive authority over courts in their jurisdictions. Not only did they appoint most judges, but they appointed them without life tenure; that guarantee of independence from executive influence, which Parliament had provided for the mother country in 1701, did not extend to the colonies. This was understandable, since colonial legislatures would otherwise have completely dominated the judiciary by means of temporary salary appropriations. Local politicians still objected that their "liberties and privileges" were thus abridged, and the issue often had to be resolved by informal compromise, after intricate negotiations between a governor and his assembly. In 1761, the Privy Council restricted such maneuvers with an order that flatly prohibited the issuance of judicial commissions unless they specified tenure upon "the pleasure of the crown."

Royal governors appointed other judges who more dependably eluded the control of local legislative leaders. Vice-admiralty courts, first authorized by act of Parliament in 1696, were convenient forums for the adjudication of disputes arising from such maritime matters as prizes, wrecks, insurance, contracts, and wages. They were single-judge courts that sat without juries, however, and their jurisdiction in the colonies ranged beyond routine maritime law to include enforcement of imperial trade regulations and the White Pine Acts. Most judges were technically commissioned by letters patent from the High Court of Admiralty in the mother country, but in fact it was the royal governors—acting in their capacity as vice-admirals of their respective provinces—who selected them. Their compensation consisted not of salaries voted by local assemblies but of fixed fees and percentage payments on the goods that they condemned. Despite the obvious commercial utility of vice-admiralty jurisdiction, it disturbed many colonists on constitutional grounds. It was "obnoxious to some . . . Gentlemen," reported one royal official in Massachusetts as early as 1706. Around midcentury, Governor William Shirley identified the economic stakes involved when he remarked that "a trial by jury here is only trying one illicit trader by his fellows, or at least by his well-wishers."

Even more controversial was another kind of gubernatorial court. This was the so-called "equitable" jurisdiction of chancery, which had emerged much earlier in the mother country to supplement the rigidly formalized "common law" of the royal courts at Westminster. Over time, England's High Court of Chancery had come to oversee an elaborate and highly technical jurisprudence of its own, dealing with problems not easily recognized in the older royal system of justice and administering relief not available there. Throughout the seventeenth century, most colonial judges had been inattentive to particular "common law" rules and so in practice had dispensed "equity" without caring or often even realizing what it was. After 1700, however, colonial governors south of New England gradually tried to establish their own chancery courts on the basis of prerogative power. Few colonists disagreed that the jurisprudence of these courts was valuable "for mitigating in many Cases the Rigour of the Laws, whose Judgments are tied down to fixed and unalterable Rules"; but many fought strenuously to prevent the introduction of a juryless system in which a governor would sit alone or with his council. Proceedings were apt to be costly, there was no appeal except to the mother country, and it was the unusual governor who had legal training. One who did, William Burnet of New York, ran his chancery court in exactly the way political opponents most feared. Using his power to subpoena delinquents, he moved vigorously in the 1720s to collect feudal rents due the Crown. This "rais'd a pretty general clamour," he acknowledged, "because it fell heavy on several Patentees." A successor, in the next decade, provoked greater hostility by questioning the very legitimacy of one important patent. Soon, it was charged, a governor would be able to make himself "master of any mans Landed Estate in the province."

After midcentury, in most places, the furor over chancery courts died down. One good reason for growing acceptance of this parallel jurisdiction was its greater utility, as colonial law developed at least some of the formal technicality associated with the older royal courts of the mother country. The trend was observable almost everywhere. As early as 1711, a statute in Connecticut imposed fines for failure to conform to rules of pleading. Citations of English precedent multiplied, as colonial libraries expanded to contain specialized treatises as well as basic manuals. Particularly in the southern colonies, the forms of legal actions were likely to imitate esoteric English prototypes. Courts were sometimes still willing to overlook defective procedures, as in 1734 when Virginia's General Court announced brusquely that an incomplete declaration was "certain enough"; but by then, a semblance of judicial rigor could be detected even in backwater areas. That same decade, the General Court of North Carolina reversed the judgment of a county court because the plaintiff's writ called on the defendant to answer one kind of action while his declaration described damages appropriate to another. In a different North Carolina case of the 1730s, a bench of county court judges listened patiently to lengthy procedural arguments until they were satisfied they "fully understood" the issues, then reversed their own judgment in part because the verdict and record of the case were "uncertain and wanted forme."

Form overlapped with substance, too, and both could touch the vital concerns of ordinary colonists in piecemeal fashion, without a crisis of the sort occasioned by the Privy Council's decision in *Winthrop v. Lechmere.* A variety of specific results might conceal an underlying pattern of change. Married women in the colonies, for example, perhaps benefited from English law requiring closer judicial scrutiny to protect their long-term interests when family property was put up for sale by their husbands. On the other hand, more generally, stricter adherence to the legal conventions of the mother country made it increasingly cumbersome for the same women to transact business on their own. In Massachusetts, just before the revolutionary era, one notably poignant proceeding indicated how the new fastidiousness in legal decision making could define and then uphold property rights against natural feelings of reciprocal justice that had once seemed appropriate to a family-based society. A married woman sued a sheriff for attaching her clothing to meet her husband's debts. Thomas Hutchinson, chief justice of the Superior Court, was sympathetic—urging that it was "safer to verge towards Conveniency" and place the woman's clothing in the recognizably exempt category of "necessary" household goods. His colleagues disagreed, however, in the name of a dubious legal orthodoxy that not incidentally was advantageous to every creditor in the colony. The case "was very hard upon the Wife," they admitted, but clothing was "personal Property" considered to "become the Husbands on Marriage."

The growing tendency toward formalism in law, evident from colony to colony, was due to the influence not only of resident imperial officialdom but of an emerging and self-conscious legal profession. That profession was itself a creation of commerce and empire. Up and down the coast, it was apparent that opportunities for successful and respectable legal careers were multiplying, as mercantile activity became more complex and predictable rules were needed to resolve disputes within court systems remodeled along English lines. On behalf of merchants overseas as well as those in the major port towns, lawyers pressed suits deep into some inland areas in order to recover money due on different instruments of credit. The most enterprising practitioners aimed for a share of vice-admiralty litigation, where the value of ships and cargoes in question determined counsel's fees, which were disproportionately high compared with the schedules established by provincial assemblies.

Imperial officials acted to promote professionalism in law. During the first two decades of the eighteenth century, for instance, royal governors of Massachusetts used their powers of appointment to improve systematically the caliber of provincial judges, who in turn demanded greater precision of lawyers practicing in their courtrooms. By the early 1730s, three well-trained English lawyers—one of whom was William Shirley, later a royal governor—were setting the tone of the profession in Boston. In Virginia, toward the beginning of the same decade, an English barrister serving as attorney general finally managed to introduce a law that prohibited anyone from pleading another person's cause without having first been examined in Williamsburg and licensed by the governor. After midcentury, particularly in more sophisticated jurisdictions, imperial officials urged lawyers to adopt the ceremonial trappings of the profession in the mother country. In 1762, Chief Justice Hutchinson ordered judges and practitioners in Massachusetts to wear English robes and gowns. Two years afterward, the Supreme Court of Judicature in New York made similar arrangements, observing that it was the "usage of most of the Civilized Nations in Europe to distinguish the different Orders of Men in the learned Professions by their Dress."

Little such encouragement was needed by then, however, as a would-be mandarin class grew in numbers and assertiveness. It had become clear to sons of the colonial gentry that a career in law was not necessarily incompatible with elevated social rank. Such a career might also produce a professional income exceeding £1,000 annually. As time passed, the infiltration of American-born gentlemen into the profession enhanced its status for others of like background. Some, most often from southern colonies, traveled to London for the prestige of training at the Inns of Court, but this was by no means a social requirement, except perhaps in the cosmopolitan environment of Charleston, South Carolina. A more widely imitated model of professional recruitment was exemplified in the colony of New York during the 1740s, when a young man named William Livingston—brought up in "ease and affluence" on Livingston Manor, the seat of a great provincial family—chose after graduating from college to enter law through the route of local apprenticeship.

Much like the royal officials around whom they tended to congregate, leading colonial lawyers eager to promote their credentials as members of a learned profession were quick to deride the crudities of locally administered justice. Distinguishing themselves ostentatiously from the mass of poorly trained practitioners, they championed the cause of legal reform. So, in his home town of Braintree, Massachusetts, John Adams tried to suppress "dirty and ridiculous Litigations" fomented by a "multiplicity of Petty foggers." So, in New York, William Livingston attacked "Low Characters" who would arise out of "obscurity and Silence" to present themselves as "sage and infallible Oracles of the Law" (see Documents, pp. 116–119). So, in Virginia, reputable lawyers complained of "ignorant Pratlers" practicing in the countryside; the "known Rules" of

English law were "not within the Reach of every common Capacity." Proposals abounded in the various colonies to improve the educational qualifications of lawyers and judges. Leading lawyers organized themselves into associations that sought to regulate admission to the bar, reduce inefficiency in the courts, and prevent competitive fee cutting. Law as a professional career would be set apart from those customary structures of governance that seventeenth-century colonists had so valued. Law would reflect the cultural perspective of provincial elites whose identity had been shaped by involvement in the commercial and political networks of empire.

But unresolved contradictions within the colonial social environment, around and after midcentury, hindered fulfillment of the highest professional aspirations in law. For one thing, even where the titles designating the superior and inferior ranks of the English legal profession were in use, there was insufficient legal business in the colonies to support functional divisions of practice according to the model of the mother country. The formal training of a colonial "barrister" might not differ from that of a colonial "attorney" or "solicitor." On the basis of lengthier practical experience, some lawyers in some colonial jurisdictions earned the exclusive right to be called "barristers" and to appear as advocates in courts of superior jurisdiction; but even the most prominent had also to engage in precisely the routine work outside the courtroom—such as debt collection—that occupied inferior practitioners in England. Just to obtain one's fees from so unspecialized and dispersed a practice was tedious and unedifying. Thomas Jefferson, ever offended by the grinding realities of professional life, barely received 50 percent of what was owed him.

Then, too, the standing of lawyers in provincial society was not quite high enough to suit their ambitious purposes. In the southern colonies, lawyers were conspicuous alongside merchants and others hoping to push their way into the gentry class by purchasing cheap interior land. Established planters affecting to be natural gentlemen, whether trained in law or not, felt threatened by such intruders and so were quick to dismiss them as "mercenary Advisors." Among wealthy merchants in the major port towns to the north, there was lingering suspicion of legal expertise, which seemed expensive and time-consuming compared with informal trade procedures for the arbitration of disputes. Proud men of commerce also resented the intellectual pretensions of lawyers, especially where—as in New

York—the elite sector of the profession was allied with large landed interests. In New England, above all, there was still an important rival profession to contend with. A "reverend orator" of Boston might appear enough a gentleman to sport "a diamond ring and a white handkerchief." After the Great Awakening convulsed the region in the early 1740s, ancient Puritan prejudices against the legal profession revived; the aura of superior virtue that surrounded the clerical calling continued to make an impression on scrupulous New Englanders.

About the same time, almost everywhere in colonial America, lawyers were entering politics in significant numbers. Here it was that the ambiguities of their situation became most troublesome. Some could hope to move in and out of various Crown offices; but the apparatus and patronage of empire remained too underdeveloped to entice most of them into signing up loyally as friends of prerogative power. Many drifted into the opposite political camp. Because "the road both to power and wealth passes entirely through the channel of the People in this province," observed one Pennsylvanian at the middle of the century, "Our lawyers are such very prudent Gentlemen that they will not hazard their interest with them." For professional lawyers to make a go of being popular politicians, however, might call for delicate footwork on their part. Much of their everyday legal business, after all, consisted of harassing debtors and delinquent tenants. In 1761, the printer of a German-language newspaper in Pennsylvania pointed out how harmful it could be to elect lawyers to the provincial Assembly, "because what is to their profit is often to the farmers' loss." Further, as legislators, lawyers vastly complicated statutes that in former days had been "straight and simple with nothing much to discuss about." It was surprising, according to this printer, that some "people in the distant counties" were "so much in love with the city-people." In fact, out in the hinterland there was no great upsurge of grassroots enthusiasm for learned professional leadership. Localistic hostility toward lawyers, often tinged by pietism, was much in evidence. One cautionary tale printed in the *Virginia Almanac* of 1762 ended with a line that elegantly outlined the larger geography of antiprofessional sentiment: "I know not . . . what Distinction there may be made in *London*; but I am sure, by sad Experience, *we in the Country know no difference between* a Lawyer *and a* Lyar."

To achieve success on the political stage, John Adams once confided to his diary, he would have to "attempt some uncommon, unexpected enterprise in law." He had to "look out for a cause to speak to, and . . . cut a flash, strike amazement, to catch the vulgar." The most appealing strategy, for a lawyer in search of opportunities for grand popular performance, was to challenge executive authority. This had been the way of Philadelphia's Andrew Hamilton, when he journeyed to New York in 1735 to secure an acquittal in a prosecution for seditious libel against John Peter Zenger, printer for an antigubernatorial faction. "Is it not surprising," Hamilton asked the jury, "to see a subject, upon his receiving a commission from the King to be a governor of a colony in America, immediately imagining himself to be vested with all the prerogatives belonging to the sacred person of his Prince?" Hamilton triumphed in the particular instance, to the applause of an assembled throng, although it was perfectly clear to professional lawyers—among whom he was happy to count himself—that he had neither cited nor established any sound precedent for "liberty of the press." All the Zenger case proved was that a colonial jury would probably refuse to punish anyone for publishing honest criticism of a governor and his allies; similar criticism of local legislators could still be risky. This mattered little to the New York crowd. "If it is not law," exclaimed one of Hamilton's admirers, "it is better than law, it ought to be law, and will always be law wherever justice prevails." Two years later, a disgusted barrister in Barbados produced a stinging rebuttal to Hamilton's argument. One reason for bothering to do so, he explained, was to preserve "the dignity of the profession of the law in these remote parts of the British dominions; and prevent its learned professors in England . . . from suspecting that all their American brethren use the like arts to gain popularity."

Some three decades after the Zenger case, John Adams revealed even more compellingly the curious configurations of colonial politics that led some professionalized lawyers to champion popular causes as orators of liberty. The son of a prosperous shoemaker and farmer who had risen within the social hierarchy of small-town New England, Adams as a young man gave long thought to becoming a minister before he settled on a career in law. Once the decision had been made, his ambitions in the profession were unbounded. "How greatly elevated, above common People, and above Divines is this

Lawyer," he exulted after listening to one local luminary. What might frustrate the purposes of so relentless a personality? In Massachusetts, the answer was obvious. The extensive clan of one man, Thomas Hutchinson, was usurping power not only in the political arena as a whole but within the narrower legal world as well. Hutchinson himself was both lieutenant governor of the province and chief justice, having attained the latter position with no formal training in law and only minor judicial experience. So in 1765, Adams sat down to compose an angry closet oration in his diary. Its Ciceronian style suggests that this driving provincial lawyer saw himself in a climactic struggle with nothing less than a latter-day American version of the Roman tyrant Catiline:

> Has not his Honour . . . discovered to the People in innumerable Instances, a very ambitious and avaricious Disposition? Has he not grasped four of the most important offices in the Province into his own Hands? Has not his Brother in Law Oliver another of the greatest Places in Government? Is not a Brother of the Secretary, a Judge of the Superiour Court? Has not that Brother a son in the House? Has not his secretary a son in the House, who is also a Judge in one of the Counties? Did not that son marry the daughter of another of the Judges of the Superiour Court? Has not the Lieutenant Governor a Brother, a Judge of the Pleas in Boston? and a Namesake and near Relation who is another Judge? Has not the Lieutenant Governor a near Relation who is Register of his own Court of Probate?

As question followed question, Adams's fury increased. "Is not this amazing ascendancy of one Family," he concluded, "Foundation sufficient on which to erect a Tyranny? Is it not enough to excite Jealousies among the People?"

Here, then, was the setting for the familiar and fast-moving developments of the tumultuous revolutionary decade. Some prominent lawyers, many quite young, joined a movement threatening to undermine the empire that had sustained their professional identity. Others, generally somewhat older and likely to be connected with the imperial establishment, held back or openly backed the Tory cause. John Adams reported that three of his best friends had been "seduced from his bosom" by the blandishments of Chief Justice Hutchinson. For the most part, those who became revolutionaries did so with unease. Trained to respect legal forms, they were reluctant to endorse radical demands that judges do business as usual in flagrant violation of the Stamp Act, although the alternative of closing down the courts sharply reduced their professional incomes. And they agonized over the weaknesses of their shifting constitutional position, which was associated with the radical fringe in the mother country and which ignored or contradicted orthodox principles of public law that they knew to be the legacy of the Glorious Revolution. Time and again, Tory ideologues such as Hutchinson reminded them that representation in Parliament was "virtual," not "actual," each member being expected to consult the interest of the realm; that parliamentary statutes were a part of the English constitution and uncontrollable by other law or power; that sovereignty could not be somehow divided, between the mother country and the colonies, without producing the "monstrous" absurdity of *imperium in imperio*. "There is no alternative," explained one English spokesman, "either the colonies are a part of the community of Great Britain or they are in a state of nature with respect to her."

The latter possibility was alarming to many American lawyers. In his *Letters from a Farmer in Pennsylvania*, the most widely circulated revolutionary tract before Tom Paine's *Common Sense*, John Dickinson chose to survey the political scene at the end of 1767 without identifying himself as a professional lawyer and spoke darkly of the "storm" and "calamities" that might ensue if protest were not "sedate" as well as "fervent" (see Documents, pp. 119–123). His concern was justified. Before the decade was over, a New York election campaign would resound to the slogan—"no lawyer in the Assembly." Insurgents in the North Carolina back country would soon echo that cry: "There should be no Lawyers in the province, they damned themselves if there should." And an angered citizenry in Monmouth County, New Jersey, would denounce "the uncircumcised L——yrs" as "Private Leaches, sucking out our very Hearts Blood" (see Documents, pp. 123–126). If professionalized lawyers did not make haste to lead the Revolution, possibly they would be numbered among its victims.

Within a few years, the rush of events decided the issue, as English politicians compounded the folly of their original revenue measures by heavy-handed efforts to suppress resistance. Half a century of continual friction with imperial officialdom had prepared colonists to respond bitterly when customs inspectors swarmed along the coast and the government in the mother country attempted to enlarge further the prerogative element in colonial courts at the expense of jury trials and judicial independence. By 1775 there was no turning back, and legal ideologues of the revolutionary movement had finally formulated the constitutional theory that would accompany the last steps toward independence. Such terms as "British Empire," argued John Adams, were the language of "court sycophants." There was no "Empire," and never had been. The first colonists had not simply carried along their legal "birthright" when they "discovered" the American continent; they had founded separate new societies outside the realm. They had then voluntarily reassociated with the king, loyalty to whom was what still loosely linked the English-speaking world. If the king and his ministers persisted in violating the terms of agreement by which this reunion had supposedly been achieved, there was no reason for the mainland American "states" to hesitate in going their own way once again.

Thomas Jefferson and Alexander Hamilton as well as John Adams argued along such lines. In its historical and metaphorical content, however, this was primarily the theory of New Englanders—not just of lawyers but of clergymen and others who occupied the public forum of the region. It was much the same theory, indeed, that had been espoused in the days of Edmund Andros. Here was a proper point of reference, as lawyers made the ultimate case for Revolution. However professionalized, they adopted a constitutional vocabulary that resonated to popular traditions. New Englanders, particularly, knew what it meant to have left the realm, understanding as they did the entire history of Protestantism as a drama of repeated separations or withdrawals from corruption. And they knew what it meant to have established their own small societies in the New World, having labored long and hard to make them work. Jefferson himself, critical of oligarchy in Virginia, conceived of an alternative system in terms that recalled the Puritan town meeting. A constitutional argument based on social compact and attuned to the religious idealism of an earlier age could appeal in New England as nowhere else. If the legal principles of revolutionary leaders were unsound by English standards, they made special sense in a region with so strong a Nonconformist and communal heritage.

What would happen afterward was another matter. In June of 1776, at Ipswich, the judges of a reconstituted Massachusetts Superior Court exhibited their new commissions and delivered a formal grand jury charge composed by Chief Justice John Adams, then in

Philadelphia representing his state. It was "an appeal to the conservative principles of the people," according to Adams. It explained the social compact, recently broken, and went on to demand enforcement of the laws—to preserve "peace, virtue, and good order." Seemingly, little had changed over the previous century and a half. The challenge of erecting a new polity would test the relevance and staying power of New England's traditions, and determine their influence within the evolving constitutional system of the United States of America.

Documents

Introduction

The materials that follow have been chosen to amplify, and to provide opportunities for discussion of, various points raised in the preceding essay. The governing principle of selection has been accessibility to the general reader. This has required exclusion of some kinds of evidence and some issues that legal historians rightly consider important. It has also dictated a cautiously flexible policy of making minor modifications in the original texts where otherwise the meaning might be lost because of archaic spelling, punctuation, or syntax. Such editing has been kept to a minimum, however, since irregularities in language often reveal the vernacular sources of early American law. In the interest of readability, there is no scholarly apparatus here to identify textual variations, although ellipses are used throughout to show that substantial sections have been omitted. The headnotes indicate where anyone should go who wishes to consult complete and exact versions of particular documents.

I.

Indian and English Ideas of Property

The process of mutual adaptation by which Indians and whites borrowed one another's vocabulary and procedures could be quite incomplete and superficial. In the negotiation reproduced below, an eighteenth-century Iroquois leader named Canassateego referred to the receipt of goods "in Consideration" of the "Release" of land belonging to his people, which from an English point of view meant that the goods were to be regarded as full payment in a contractual exchange recognized and guaranteed by law. Canassateego also made a claim to territory by "Right of Conquest." At the same time, presenting the grievances of his people and requesting additional goods, he articulated or implied other standards of "Justice" applicable to the situation. Were these traditional Indian ideas consistent with white ideas? In his reply, the lieutenant governor of Pennsylvania was at some pains to appear responsive to tribal protocol. But did he make any important concessions to the alternative concepts of property that had surfaced in Canassateego's speech? The discussion here occurred at a relatively late and unfortunate stage in the history of Indian–white relations in Pennsylvania. With William Penn long gone from the scene, aggressive traders and land-hungry settlers from England and continental Europe had effectively dispossessed the Delawares. Led by James Logan, the provincial secretary, local officials had succeeded in enlisting the Iroquois as allies in this campaign.

SPEECHES OF CANASSATEEGO FOR THE SIX NATIONS AND LIEUTENANT GOVERNOR GEORGE THOMAS OF PENNSYLVANIA (July 7, 1742)*

Canassateego:

BRETHREN, the Governor and Council, and all present,

According to our Promise we now propose to return you an Answer to the several Things mentioned to us Yesterday, and shall beg Leave to speak to publick Affairs first, tho' they were what you spoke to last. On this Head you Yesterday put us in Mind, first, of William Penn's early and constant Care to cultivate Friendship with all the Indians; of the Treaty we held with one of his Sons, about ten Years ago; and of the Necessity there is at this Time of keeping the Roads between us clear and free from all Obstructions. We are all

* Printed by Cadwallader Colden in *The History of the Five Indian Nations of Canada* (London, 1747); reprinted in Wilcomb E. Washburn (ed.), *The Indian and the White Man* (Garden City, N.Y., 1964), pp. 329–334.

very sensible of the kind Regard that good Man William Penn had for all the Indians, and cannot but be pleased to find that his Children have the same. We well remember the Treaty you mention, held with his Son on his Arrival here, by which we confirmed our League of Friendship, that is to last as long as the Sun and Moon endure. In Consequence of this, we, on our Part, shall preserve the Road free from all Incumbrances; in Confirmation whereof we lay down this String of Wampum.

You in the next Place said you would enlarge the Fire and make it burn brighter, which we are pleased to hear you mention; and we assure you, we shall do the same, by adding to it more Fuel, that it may still flame out more strongly than ever. In the last Place, you were pleased to say that we are bound by the strictest Leagues, to watch for each others Preservation; that we should hear with our Ears for you, and you hear with your Ears for us. This is equally agreeable to us; and we shall not fail to give you early Intelligence, whenever any Thing of Consequence comes to our Knowledge. And to encourage you to do the same, and to nourish in your Hearts what you have spoke to us with your Tongues, about the Renewal of our Amity and the Brightening of the Chain of Friendship, we confirm what we have said with another Belt of Wampum.

BRETHREN, we received from the Proprietor Yesterday, some Goods in Consideration of our Release of the Lands on the West-side of the Susquehannah. It is true, we have the full Quantity according to Agreement; but if the Proprietor had been here himself, we think, in Regard of our Numbers and Poverty, he would have made an Addition to them. If the Goods were only to be divided amongst the Indians present, a single Person would have but a small Portion; but if you consider what Numbers are left behind, equally entitled with us to a Share, there will be extremely little. We therefore desire, if you have the Keys of the Proprietor's Chest, you will open it, and take out a little more for us.

We know our Lands are now become more valuable. The white People think we do not know their Value; but we are sensible that the Land is everlasting, and the few Goods we receive for it are soon worn out and gone. For the future, we will sell no Lands but when the Proprietor is in the Country; and we will know beforehand, the Quantity of the Goods we are to receive. Besides, we are not well used with respect to the Lands still unsold by us. Your People daily settle on these Lands, and spoil our Hunting. We must insist on your removing them, as you know they have no Right to settle to the Northward of Kittochtinny-Hills. In particular, we renew our Complaints against some People who are settled at the Juniata, a Branch of the Susquehannah, and all the Banks of that River, as far as Mahaniay; and we desire they may be forthwith made to go off the Land, for they do great Damage to our Cousins the Delawares.

We have further to observe, with respect to the Lands lying on the West-side of the Susquehannah, that though the Proprietor has paid us for what his People possess, yet some Parts of that Country have been taken up by Persons, whose Place of Residence is to the South of this Province, from whom we have never received any Consideration. This Affair was recommended to you by our Chiefs at our last Treaty; and you then, at our earnest Desire, promised to write a Letter to that Person who has the Authority over those People, and to procure us his Answer. As we have never heard from you on this Head, we want to know what you have done in it. If you have not done any Thing, we now renew our Request, and desire you will inform the Person whose People are seated on our Lands, that that Country belongs to us, in Right of Conquest—we having bought it with our Blood, and taken it from our Enemies in fair War; and we expect, as Owners of that Land, to receive such a Consideration for it as the Land is worth. We desire you will press him to send a positive Answer. Let him say Yes or No. If he says Yes, we will treat with him; if No, we are able to do ourselves Justice; and we will do it, by going to take Payment ourselves.

It is customary with us to make a Present of Skins, whenever we renew our Treaties. We are ashamed to offer our Brethren so few, but your Horses and Cows have eat the Grass our Deer used to feed on. This has made them scarce, and will, we hope, plead in Excuse for our not bringing a larger Quantity. If we could have spared more, we would have given more, but we are really poor; and desire you'll not consider the Quantity, but few as they are, accept them in Testimony of our Regard.

Lieutenant Governor Thomas:
BRETHREN,
We thank you for the many Declarations of Respect you have given us, in this solemn Renewal of our Treaties. We receive, and shall keep your String and Belts of Wampum, as Pledges of your

Sincerity, and desire those we gave you may be carefully preserved, as Testimonies of ours.

In answer to what you say about the Proprietaries: they are all absent, and have taken the Keys of their Chest with them; so that we cannot, on their Behalf, enlarge the Quantity of Goods. Were they here, they might perhaps be more generous; but we cannot be liberal for them. The Government will, however, take your Request into Consideration; and in Regard to your Poverty, may perhaps made you a Present. . . .

The Number of Guns, as well as every Thing else, answers exactly with the Particulars specified in your Deed of Conveyance, which is more than was agreed to be given you. It was your own Sentiments, that the Lands on the West-side of the Susquehannah, were not so valuable as those on the East; and an Abatement was to be made, proportionable to the Difference in Value. But the Proprietor overlooked this, and ordered the full Quantity to be delivered, which you will look on as a Favour.

It is very true, that Lands are of late become more valuable; but what raises their Value? Is it not entirely owing to the Industry and Labour used by the white People, in their Cultivation and Improvement? Had not they come amongst you, these Lands would have been of no Use to you, any further than to maintain you. And is there not, now you have sold so much, enough left for all the Purposes of Living? What you say of the Goods, that they are soon worn out, is applicable to every Thing; but you know very well, that they cost a great deal of Money; and the Value of Land is no more, than it is worth in Money.

On your former Complaints against People's settling the Lands on the Juniata, and from thence all along on the Susquehannah as far as Mahaniay, some Magistrates were sent expressly to remove them, and we thought no Persons would presume to stay after that.

(Here they interrupted the Lieutenant Governor, and said: "These Persons who were sent did not do their Duty. So far from removing the People, they made Surveys for themselves, and they are in League with the Trespassers. We desire more effectual Methods may be used, and honester Persons employed." Which the Lieutenant Governor promised, and then proceeded.)

BRETHREN, according to the Promise made at our last Treaty with you, Mr. Logan did write to the Governor of Maryland, that he might make you Satisfaction for such of your Lands as his People had taken up, but did not receive one Word from him upon that Head. I will write to him again, and endeavour to procure you a satisfactory Answer. We do not doubt that he will do you Justice. But we exhort you to be careful not to exercise any Acts of Violence towards his People, as they likewise are our Brethren, and Subjects of the same great King; and therefore Violence towards them, must be productive of very evil Consequences.

I shall conclude what I have to say at this Time, with Acknowledgments for your Present, which is very agreeable to us, from the Expressions of Regard used by you in Presenting it—Gifts of this Nature receiving their Value from the Affection of the Giver, and not from the Quantity or Price of the Thing given.

II.

Toward a Definition of Slavery

The following statute, passed by Maryland in 1664, illustrates the tentativeness with which Chesapeake legislators approached the problem of slavery. Stipulating that all slaves would serve "Durante Vita" (for life), this law was a major step in the transition from a labor system based primarily on white servitude for limited terms to one that relied on perpetual ownership of blacks. The General Assembly of the colony would soon make explicit a premise simply implied here: conversion to Christianity did not alter the status or obligations of a slave. As of 1664, however, blacks were not numerous in Maryland, and it is apparent that the legislature was groping toward a formula to suit a highly uncertain future. Although a presumption was firmly established that every black in the colony would serve for life, the first two sentences of the statute suggested that the condition of slavery might extend to Indians and perhaps some others who were not black. To what extent does the subsequent language of the statute accord with this formula? How far did this legislation go toward defining slavery in purely racial terms? It is noteworthy that Maryland's lawmakers here adopted the principle that paternal status determined the status of children. This later yielded to the prevailing rule of American slave law, by which maternal status was determinative. What possibly did legislators in Maryland hope to achieve, as of 1664, by emphasizing paternal status? Why, as time went on, would the rule followed here have come to appear less practical than its opposite?

MARYLAND GENERAL ASSEMBLY: AN ACT CONCERNING NEGROES & OTHER SLAVES (1664)*

Bee itt Enacted by the Right Honourable the Lord Proprietary, by the advice and Consent of the upper and lower house of this present Generall Assembly, That all Negroes or other slaves already within the Province And all Negroes and other slaves to bee hereafter imported into the Province shall serve Durante Vita. And all Children born of any Negro or other slave shall be Slaves as their ffathers were for the terme of their lives. And forasmuch as divers freeborne English women forgettfull of their free Condition and to the disgrace of our Nation doe intermarry with Negro Slaves, by which alsoe divers suites may arise touching the Issue of such woemen and a great damage doth befall the Masters of such Negros—for prevention whereof and for deterring such freeborne women from such shamefull Matches, Bee itt further Enacted by the Authority advice and Consent aforesaid, That whatsoever free borne woman shall inter marry with any slave from and after the Last day of this present Assembly shall Serve the master of such slave dureing the life of her husband, And that all the Issue of such freeborne woemen soe marryed shall be Slaves as their fathers were. And Bee itt further Enacted that all the Issues of English or other freeborne woemen that have already marryed Negroes shall serve the Masters of their Parents till they be Thirty yeares of age and noe longer.

III.

Citizenship and Politics

Amid its elaborate catalogue of injustices, the Declaration of Independence would charge George III with "obstructing the laws for naturalization of foreigners." The rights of aliens had previously stirred political controversy in the colonies, as the following argument indicates. It was formulated in 1758 by Daniel Dulany, Maryland's outstanding lawyer and a prominent figure in the upper house of the Assembly there. Late that year, the lower house had passed a law to validate all titles acquired by or from unnaturalized Protestant

---

* *The legislation of 1664 is available in William Hand Browne et al. (eds.),* Archives of Maryland *(Baltimore, 1883–), 1, 533–534, and has been reprinted in Willie Lee Rose (ed.),* A Documentary History of Slavery in North America *(New York, 1976), p. 24.*

landholders in the province. Those who stood to benefit most immediately were the German-speaking people of western Maryland. On the other hand, unscrupulous real estate operators stood to lose if titles deriving from the transactions of aliens were protected against the challenge of an "escheat" warrant. Such a challenge could result in temporary reversion of the contested property to the lord proprietary, after which the challenging party might secure a new patent and thus complete the process of dispossessing the original landholder. Mindful of proprietary rights, the upper house voted against reform, whereupon Dulany entered his dissenting opinion in the official record. Along with many of his colleagues, he had objected to the failure of the bill in question to include local Roman Catholics, but that problem was overshadowed by the issues outlined below. What were the elements of Dulany's argument that tended to broaden the plight of aliens into a potentially popular cause appealing to English settlers as well? What would have been the constitutional implications of similar reasoning advanced in a royal colony where ultimately it was the king whose right to "escheats" was at stake?

DANIEL DULANY IN THE UPPER HOUSE OF THE MARYLAND GENERAL ASSEMBLY (December 1758)*

The question being put, whether the Bill sent up from the Lower House entituled "an Act for the Security of purchasers and others Claiming by or from protestant Aliens" should pass and determined in the negative: To that negative I Dissent and desire that my Dissent with the following reasons for it may be entered.

1. Because Aliens who have settled in this Province, and by their Labour Industry & Frugality improved a Wilderness into regular Fruitful and well stocked Plantations, were invited hither by Proclamations Translated into the German Language and Carefully Dispersed in Germany; and the Faith of this Government, which ought to be religiously observed, hath been in the most solemn and explicit Terms engaged to them that they should be secure and protected in the enjoyment of their property.

2. Because the miscarriage of the Bill upon an apprehension that his Lordship the Lord proprietary might Dislike it, from the Consideration of his Revenues being affected in respect of his Escheats, implies a supposition too Derogatory to his Lord-

* *Archives of Maryland*, 56, 56–59.

ships Honour and apparently repugnant to experience, as well as a rule too narrow and inconsistent with the Dignity of the Upper House of the Legislature, to be admitted or suffered.

3. Because the Rights of Aliens acquired upon the most meritorious Considerations were to be destroyed impeached or brought into Hazards for the delusive Prospect of a temporary Increase of his Lordships Revenues, and many Hundred Families of usefull industrious and well affected Subjects would be effectually Banished and others under their Circumstances Certainly prevented by Such a flagrant Violation of the Rules of good Faith and Justice from Settling here, to the real Diminution of his Lordships Revenue, the disgrace of his Government and the Impoverishment of his Province.

4. Because such a Bill (it having been the Subject of Deliberation and publick Debate) is now become Absolutely necessary to quiet the minds of the Alien Inhabitants who might be intimidated into a surrender of their Rights upon the Issuing of Escheat Warrants from their Ignorance of our Laws and Constitution, a Consciousness of their Inability to manage Law suits with the Same Advantage that others can, or a dread of Power; or if this should not happen, those who may be tempted by the Bait of Escheat warrants would be ensnared by the alluring Prospect of gain . . . to vindicate and Support these oppressive Escheats. If the Case of an Alien patentee who has . . . paid his respective fees and punctually rendered to his Lordship the reserved Quit Rents as his immediate Tenant, were stated in a special verdict, I cant Conceive that any purchaser under an Escheat Patent could finally prevail (should the Aliens pretentions be effectually prosecuted) against such an Alien by a rigorous Determination contrary to the rules of Publick Faith, and the sacred Obligations of equity and Justice.

5. Because if the principle upon which the Bill has been rejected, should be extended to similar Cases (and no reason can be assigned why it should not), it will become a rule not to give a passage through this House to any Bill securitative of the rights of the People, as the Lord Proprietary might be affected in his Escheats in proportion to the utility and efficacy of such a Bill, and thus one of the great ends of Legislature would be defeated and a Destruction pregnant with irreconcileable Enmity be established between his Lordships and the Tenants

Interest, which ought for their mutual Advantage and Benefit to be Inseparably conjoined; and such Jealousies and Suspicions, Dissentions and Annimosities as cited cant but prove highly Detrimental to his Lordships revenue, discourage the further Settlement of this province, cast an odious Blemish upon the Character of his Government, and depopulate the Country.

6. Because such Bills have passed into Laws in the other Colonies, Particularly in New York Pensilvania and Virginia, and the want of such a provision here will deprive this province of the Benefit accruing to the other Colonies from their better Policy in this Article, for the Situation and Circumstances of the Inhabitants of this Country (except a few Mechanicks) are such that they cant Subsist without the Allowance of Some portion of real Property, and Aliens are not Naturalized by "the Act of Parliament for naturalizing of Foreign Protestants" till after a residence in the Plantations for a Term of Years. Should there not be that assurance given them here which they have in the other Colonies, Arising from Acts of Assembly having a Relation or Retrospect to Confirm their Titles when by the Act of God they may be hindered from Strictly Complying with all the Terms of the Statute, it is not reasonably to be expected that any of these Emigrants will settle here.

7. Because the Miscarriage of the Bill in this House may set greedy men upon Disturbing the Possessions of Aliens from an Expectation of the Countenance of the Government, and should any of these Alien Inhabitants be hereafter naturalized (which depends upon the Probable Contingency of their Living the Time required by the Statute), after being Stripped of their Possessions for want of knowledge or ability or a defect of Spirit to defend their Rights, they might recover their Lands against Escheat Patentees from the Legal Operation of their Naturalization, and great oppression Confusion and multiplicity of Law Suites and other Inconveniencies may ensue.

8. Because a Law to the effect of the rejected Bill would Advance his Lordships and his Noble Ancestors Laudable endeavours to settle this part of his Majestys Dominions with usefull and industrious Subjects and add great weight to the Late Generous "Instructions for the Encouragement of Aliens"; but no

promise no invitation no proclamation no Instruction will, after the Miscarriage of this Bill, be regarded but as an engine or Snare to catch and ruin the unwary.

9. Lastly, because the suggestion is as groundless as the apprehension is Chimerical, that if this Bill were passed into a Law some expressions artificially inserted in it may possibly introduce rule of Determination in the Courts of Law tending to invalidate his Lordships General Right in the matter of Escheats, and if there were Really such expressions they ought to be pointed out and corrected & not Assigned as a reason for rejecting the whole Bill. The Composition of the Bill is so Concise and plain, and the subject Matter of it so Confined and Simple, that the Dread of any Intent Design in the Framers of it Seems to be rather the effect of an excessive Diffidence than a prudent Caution.

IV.
A Radical View of Colonization

To agree that English colonists had "discovered" vacant lands in North America still left room for disagreement about the extent to which English law bound the colonies. Eventually, under the pressure of revolutionary events, some Americans developed a mythic account of their early history that postulated the creation of separate political entities outside the realm (see Essay, pp. 66–67). To fill out their new historical insight into the meaning of American sovereignty, Patriot ideologues reinterpreted the legal process by which settlers from the mother country had occupied territory in the New World. Perhaps the most striking statement of such revised doctrine appeared in a set of resolutions that Thomas Jefferson prepared for the Virginia Convention of August 1774 to guide the colony's delegates at the first Continental Congress. Because of illness, Jefferson was unable to attend the convention, but his admirers quickly arranged publication under the now familiar title: A Summary View of the Rights of British America *(Williamsburg, 1774). Somewhat like seventeenth-century Puritans, Jefferson made no specific effort to trace rights in American land either to the Indians or to the king of England. Although he spoke of "conquest," is it clear whether this referred to struggle with native populations rather than with Europeans or the physical environment? Reflecting a theme that was fashionable in some English circles, he insisted that land in America resembled Saxon holdings "of the Allodial nature"—that is, free from feudal obligations. In contrast to the Puritans, who justified their possession of American soil by citing the "promise" of God to a special "people," Jefferson implied that title to land might ultimately be derived from "natural right." Insofar as such a "right" inhered in "civil institutions," how could it be differentiated from the raw "might" that in fact had overwhelmed Indian claims? How willing was Jefferson to affirm the "right" of an individual over and against the demands of political society?*

THOMAS JEFFERSON: DRAFT OF INSTRUCTIONS TO THE VIRGINIA DELEGATES IN THE CONTINENTAL CONGRESS (July 1774)*

Resolved that it be an instruction to the said deputies when assembled in General Congress with the deputies from the other states of British America to propose to the said Congress that an humble and dutiful address be presented to his majesty begging leave to lay before him as chief magistrate of the British empire the united complaints of his majesty's subjects in America; complaints which are excited by many unwarrantable incroachments and usurpations, attempted to be made by the legislature of one part of the empire, upon those rights which god and the laws have given equally and independently to all. . . . And in order that these our rights, as well as the invasions of them, may be laid more fully before his majesty, to take a view of them from the origin and first settlement of these countries.

To remind him that our ancestors, before their emigration to America, were the free inhabitants of the British dominions in Europe, and possessed a right, which nature has given to all men, of departing from the country in which chance, not choice has placed them, of going in quest of new habitations, and of there establishing new societies, under such laws and regulations as to them shall seem most likely to promote public happiness. That their Saxon ancestors had under this universal law, in like manner, left their native wilds and woods in the North of Europe, had possessed themselves of the island of Britain then less charged with inhabitants, and had established there that system of laws which has so long been the glory and protection of that country. Nor was ever any claim of superiority or dependence asserted over them by that mother country from

---

* Excerpted from the manuscript version of *A Summary View*, which has been printed in many editions of Jefferson's writings, including Julian P. Boyd et al. (eds.), *The Papers of Thomas Jefferson* (Princeton, N.J., 1950–), 1, 121–137.

which they had migrated: and were such a claim made it is believed his majesty's subjects in Great Britain have too firm a feeling of the rights derived to them from their ancestors to bow down the sovereignty of their state before such visionary pretensions. And it is thought that no circumstance has occurred to distinguish materially the British from the Saxon emigration. America was conquered, and her settlements made and firmly established, at the expence of individuals, and not of the British public. Their own blood was spilt in acquiring lands for their settlement, their own fortunes expended in making that settlement effectual. For themselves they fought, for themselves they conquered, and for themselves alone they have right to hold. . . .

That we shall at this time also take notice of an error in the nature of our landholdings, which crept in at a very early period of our settlement. The introduction of the Feudal tenures into the kingdom of England, though antient, is well enough understood to set this matter in a proper light. In the earlier ages of the Saxon settlement feudal holdings were certainly altogether unknown, and very few, if any, had been introduced at the time of the Norman conquest. Our Saxon ancestors held their lands, as they did their personal property, in absolute dominion, disencumbered with any superior, answering nearly to the nature of those possessions which the Feudalists term Allodial: William the Norman first introduced that system generally. The lands which had belonged to those who fell in the battle of Hastings, and in the subsequent insurrections of his reign, formed a considerable proportion of the lands of the whole kingdom. These he granted out, subject to feudal duties, as did he also those of a great number of his new subjects, who by persuasions or threats were induced to surrender them for that purpose. But still much was left in the hands of his Saxon subjects, held of no superior, and not subject to feudal conditions. These therefore by express laws, enacted to render uniform the system of military defence, were made liable to the same military duties as if they had been feuds; and the Norman lawyers soon found means to saddle them also with all the other feudal burthens. But still they had not been surrendered to the king, they were not derived from his grant, and therefore they were not holden of him. A general principle indeed was introduced that 'all lands in England were held either mediately or immediately of the crown': but this was borrowed from those holdings which were truly feudal, and only applied to others for the purpose of illustration.

Feudal holdings were therefore but exceptions out of the Saxon laws of possession, under which all lands were held in absolute right. These therefore still form the basis or groundwork of the Common law, to prevail wheresoever the exceptions have not taken place. America was not conquered by William the Norman, nor its lands surrendered to him or any of his successors. Possessions there are undoubtedly of the Allodial nature. Our ancestors, however, who migrated hither, were laborers, not lawyers. The fictitious principle that all lands belong originally to the king, they were early persuaded to believe real, and accordingly took grants of their own lands from the crown. And while the crown continued to grant for small sums and on reasonable rents, there was no inducement to arrest the error and lay it open to public view. But his majesty has lately taken on him to advance the terms of purchase and of holding to the double of what they were, by which means the acquisition of lands being rendered difficult, the population of our country is likely to be checked. It is time therefore for us to lay this matter before his majesty, and to declare that he has no right to grant lands of himself. From the nature and purpose of civil institutions, all the lands within the limits which any particular society has circumscribed around itself, are assumed by that society, and subject to their allotment only. This may be done by themselves assembled collectively, or by their legislature to whom they have delegated sovereign authority; and, if they are allotted in neither of these ways, each individual of the society may appropriate to himself such lands as he finds vacant, and occupancy will give him title. . . .

V.

State Religion Extemporized

In the summer of 1619, twenty burgesses elected by Virginia's freemen met for five days with the governor of the colony and six councillors. This famous General Assembly, formed according to instructions from the London Company, enacted a variety of laws to transform the military regime of Virginia's early years into a government that replicated political features of the mother country. Among these laws were the rules of moral conduct and provisions for ecclesiastical organization listed below. Although the intention of Virginia's first legislators was to establish the Church of England in their colony and authorize it to collaborate with the state in supervising morals, they were unsure how to do so. In the absence of a bishop, the General Assembly and the governor had to formulate policies and perform duties that in the mother country would have been the responsibility of ecclesiastical officials. Local clergymen were expected to function in a judicial capacity, supported by the state; but the guidelines for such jurisdiction—perhaps expected to be imitative of England's ecclesiastical courts—were vague. For example, what were to be the procedures for hearing evidence to find guilt or innocence on particular charges? Where the role of civil government was supposed to overlap with that of the church, which kind of authority appears to have had the decisive say?

ENACTMENTS OF VIRGINIA'S GENERAL ASSEMBLY AT JAMESTOWN (July–August 1619)*

Against Idleness, gaming, drunkenness & excesse in apparel, the Assembly hath enacted as followeth:

First in detestation of idlers, be it enacted, that if any man be found to live as an Idler, though a freed man, it shall be lawful for the Incorporation or Plantation to which he belongeth to appoint him a Master to serve for wages till he shewe apparent signes of amendment.

Against gaming at Dice & cards be it ordained by this present Assembly that the winner or winners shall lose all his or their winnings & both winners and loosers shall forfeit ten shillings a man, one ten shillings whereof to goe to the discoverer, & the rest to charitable & pious uses in the Incorporation where the faults are committed.

Against drunkenes be it also decreed, that if any private person be found culpable thereof, for the first time he is to be reprooved privately by the Minister, and second time publiquely, the Third time to lye in boltes 12 houres in the House of the Provost Marshall & to paye his fees, and if he still continue in that vice, to undergo such severe punishment, as the Governor & Councell shall think fitt to be inflicted on him. But if any Officer offende in this crime, the first time he shall receive a reproof from the Governour, the second time he shall openly be reproved in the Churche by the minister, & the third time he shall first be committed & then degraded. Provided it be understood, that the Governour hath always power to restore him when he shall in his discretion thinke fitt.

* Extracted from the journal of the House of Burgesses. Organized in somewhat different form, the enactments are available in George MacLaren Brydon, *Virginia's Mother Church and the Political Conditions Under Which It Grew . . . 1607–1727* (Richmond, Va., 1947), Appendix 4, pp. 422–425.

Against excesse of apparell, that every man be assessed in the Churche for all publique contributions, if he be unmarried according to his apparell, if he be married, according to his owne & his wives or either of their apparell.

For Reformation of Swearing, every freeman and Master of a family after thrice admonition shall give 5 shillings to the use of the churche where he dwelleth: and every servant after the like admonition, except his Master discharge the fine, shall be subject to whipping. Provided that the payment of the fine notwithstanding, the said servant shall acknowledge his fault publiquely in the Church.

All persons whatever upon Sabaoth days shall frequente divine service & sermons both forenoon and afternoone; and all suche as beare armes shall bring their pieces, swordes, power, & shotte. And Every one that shall transgresse this Lawe, shall forfeit three shillinges a time to the use of the Churche, all lawful & necessary impediments excepted. But if a servant in this case shall wilfully neglecte his Masters commande he shall suffer bodily punishmente.

All Ministers in the Colony shall once a year, namely in the month of Marche, bring to the Secretary of State a true account of all Christenings, burials & marriages, upon paine, if they faile, to be censured for their negligence by the Governour & Councell. Likewise, where there be no ministers, that the commanders of the place doe supply the same duty.

No maide or woman servant, either now resident in the Colonie, or hereafter to come, shall contract herselfe in marriage without either the consente of her parents or her Master or Mistress, or of the magistrate & Minister of the place both together. And whatsoever Minister shall marry or contracte any such persons without some of the foresaid consentes shall be subjecte to the severe censure of the Governour & Counsell.

All ministers shall duely read divine service, and exercise their ministerial function according to the Ecclesiastical Lawes and orders of the church of Englande, and every Sunday in the afternoon shall Catechize suche as are not yet ripe to come to the Communion. And whosoever of them shall be found negligent or faulty in this kinde shall be subject to the censure of the Governour and Councell.

The Ministers and Churchwardens shall seeke to prevent all ungodly disorders, as suspicions of whoredoms, dishonest company keeping with weomen and such like; the committers whereofe if, upon goode admonitions and milde reproofe they will not forbeare the said skandalous offences, they are to be presented and punished accordingly.

If any person after two warnings doe not amende his or her life in point of evident suspicion of Incontinency or of the commission of any other enormous sinnes, that then he or shee shall be presented by the Church-wardens and suspended for a time from the Churche by the minister. In which interim if the same person do not amend and humbly submitt him or herselfe to the churche, he is then fully to be excommunicate, and soon after a writt or warrant is to be sente from the Governour for the apprehending of his person & seizing all his goods. Provided alwayes, that all ministers doe meet once a quarter, namely at the feast of St. Michael the Arkangell, of the nativity of our Saviour, of the Annuntiation of the blessed Virgin, and about midsomer, at James Citty or any other place where the Governour shall reside, to determine whom it is fitt to excommunicate, and that they first present their opinion to the Governour ere they proceed to the acte of excommunication.

VI.

A Blueprint for Religious Pluralism

Nowhere in America was the Church of England more delicately situated than in the royal colony of New York during the early 1750s. Anglicans there, constituting approximately one-tenth of the population, were aggressive enough to propose that money raised by public lottery for "the Advancement of Learning" be used to support a royally chartered college in which the Church of England would enjoy "a preference." In the ensuing political controversy, three young lawyers emerged to demand an institution that would not favor any particular denomination of Protestants. From the weekly columns of the Independent Reflector, *a periodical markedly influenced by English libertarian ideology, this "triumvirate" attacked Anglican pretensions and tried to spell out an alternative plan. The youngest of them was William Smith, Jr., a devout Presbyterian in his middle twenties whose father was a leader of the New York bar. Smith emphatically denied that the Church of England was established by law in the colony. In the essay excerpted below, he specified how New York's legislature should go about authorizing a truly public system of collegiate education. Precisely how much freedom did Smith intend to allow students, and faculty, within his structure of governance? Why, ultimately, did he want to make the Assembly responsible for safeguarding educational rights? Despite the enthusiastic backing of his associates, Smith's proposals were not adopted. Eventually, New York's Anglicans received a charter from the lieutenant governor and were able to open King's College in the name of the Church of England. But they had to do so without legislative approval or regular public funding. Subsequently, an odd political deal was struck by which the lottery money previously collected was divided between the new college and the Corporation of the City of New York, the latter's share having been earmarked for construction of a jail and a building to detain the crews of infected ships.*

WILLIAM SMITH, JR.:
REMARKS ON THE COLLEGE (1753)*

That a College may be a Blessing or a Curse to the Community, according to its Constitution and Government, I think appears sufficiently evident from my former Papers. That incorporating it by an Act of Assembly, will be the best Means of securing the first, and avoiding the last, is in my Opinion, equally clear and incontestible. . . . I shall now proceed to point out those Things which in my Judgment, are necessary to be inserted in the incorporating Act, for the Advancement of the true Interest of the College, and rendering it really useful to the Province. Such Things will effectually prevent its being prejudicial to the Public, and guard us against all the Mischiefs we so justly apprehend, should it ever unhappily fall into the Hands of a Party.

First: That all the Trustees be nominated, appointed, and incorporated by the Act, and that whenever an Avoidance among them shall happen, the same be reported by the Corporation to the next Sessions of Assembly, and such Vacancy supplied by Legislative Act. That they hold their Offices only at the good Pleasure of the Governor, Council and General Assembly. And that no Person of any Protestant Denomination be, on Account of his religious Persuasion, disqualified for sustaining any Office in the College. . . .

Secondly: That the President of the College be elected and deprived by a Majority of the Trustees, and all the Inferior Officers by a Majority of the Trustees with the President; and that the Election and Deprivation of the President, be always reported by the Trustees, to the next Session of Assembly, and be absolutely void, unless the Acts of the Trustees in this Matter, be then confirmed by

---

* *The Independent Reflector*, no. 21 (April 19, 1753). Along with the other numbers of the *Independent Reflector*, which were originally published unsigned but are now attributable, this one has been reprinted in Milton M. Klein (ed.), *The Independent Reflector* (Cambridge, Mass., 1963), pp. 199–205.

the Legislature. By this Means the President, who will have the supreme Superintendency of the Education of our Youth, will be kept in a continual and ultimate Dependence upon the Public; and the Wisdom of the Province being his only Support, he will have a much greater Security, in the upright Discharge of his Duty, than if he depended solely on the Trustees, who are likely to oust him of his Office and Livelihood thro' Caprice or Corruption. . . .

Thirdly: That a Majority of the President and Trustees, have Power to make By-Laws not repugnant to the Act of Incorporation, and the Law of the Land. That all such By-Laws be reported to the House of Representatives at their next succeeding Session, under the seal of the College, and the Hands of the President and five Trustees; and that if they are not reported, or being reported are not confirmed, they shall be absolutely void. . . .

Fourthly: That the Act of Incorporation contain as many Rules and Directions for the Government of the College as can be foreseen to be necessary. As all our Danger will arise from the Mis-Rule of the President and Trustees; so all our Safety consists in the Guardianship of the Legislature. . . .

The Fifth Article I propose is, that no religious Profession in particular be established in the College; but that both Officers and Scholars be at perfect Liberty to attend any Protestant Church at their Pleasure respectively. And that the Corporation be absolutely inhibited the making of any By-Laws relating to Religion, except such as compel them to attend Divine Service at some Church or other, every Sabbath, as they shall be able, lest so invaluable a Liberty be abused and *made a Cloak for Licenciousness*.

To this most important Head, I should think proper to subjoin,

Sixthly: That the whole College be every Morning and Evening convened to attend public Prayers, to be performed by the President, or in his Absence, by either of the Fellows; and that such Forms be prescribed and adhered to as all Protestants can freely join in. . . . With Respect to the Prayers, tho' I confess there are excellent Forms composed to our Hands, it would rather conduce to the Interest of our Academy, if, instead of those, new Ones were collected, which might easily be done from a Variety of approved Books of Devotion among all Sects; and perhaps it may be thought better to frame them as near as possible in the Language of Scripture. The general Forms need be but few. Occasional Parts may be made to be inserted when necessary: as in Cases of Sickness, Death, *etc.* in the College, or under general Calamities, as War, Pestilence, Drought, Floods, *etc.*, and the like as to Thanksgivings. Many of the Forms of Prayer contained in the English Liturgy, are in themselves unexceptionably good; but as establishing and imposing the Use of those, or of any other Protestant Communion, would be a discriminating Badge, it is liable to Objections, and will occasion a general Dissatisfaction. As the Introduction of them, therefore, will prejudice the College, it is a sufficient Reason against it. . . .

Seventhly: That Divinity be no Part of the public Exercises of the College. I mean, that it be not taught as a Science. That the Corporation be inhibited from electing a Divinity Professor; and that the Degrees to be conferred, be only in the Arts, Physic, and the Civil Law. Youth at a College, as I have remarked in a former Paper, are incapable of making a judicious Choice in this Matter; for this Reason the Office of a theological Professor will be useless. Besides, Principles obtruded upon their tender Minds, by the Authority of a Professor's Chair, may be dangerous. But a main Reason in support of this Clause, is the Disgust which will necessarily be given to all Parties that differ in their Professions from that of the Doctor. The Candidate for the Ministry will hereby in his Divinity Studies, whenever he is fit for them, be left to the Choice and Direction of his Parents or Guardians. . . .

Eighthly: That the Officers and Collegians have an unrestrained Access to all Books in the Library, and that free Conversation upon polemical and controverted Points in Divinity, be not discountenanced; whilst all public Disputations upon the various Tenets of different Professions of Protestants, be absolutely forbidden.

Ninthly: That the Trustees, President, and all inferior Officers, not only take and subscribe the Oaths and Declaration appointed by Statute, but be also bound by solemn Oath, in their respective Stations, to fulfil their respective Trusts, and preserve inviolate the Rights of the Scholars, according to the fundamental Rules contained in the Act. And that an Action at Law be given and well secured to every inferior Officer and Student, for every Injury against his legal Right so to be established.

And in as much as artful Intrigues may hereafter be contrived to the Prejudice of the College, and a Junto be inleagued to destroy its free Constitution, it may perhaps be thought highly expedient, that the Act contain a Clause,

Tenthly: That all future Laws, contrary to the Liberty and Fundamentals of this Act, shall be construed to be absolutely void, unless it refers to the Part thus to be altered, and expressly repeals it; and that no Act relating to the College, shall hereafter pass the House of Representatives, but with the Consent of the Majority of the whole House.

Nor would it be amiss to prescribe,

Eleventhly: That as all Contests among the inferior Officers of the College, should be finally determined by the Majority of the Members of the Corporation, so the latter should be determined in all their Disputes, by a Committee of the whole House of Representatives, or the major Part of them.

These are the Articles which in my Opinion, should be incorporated in the Act for the Establishment of the College; and without which we have the highest Reason to think, the Advantages it will produce, will at best fall short of the Expence it will create, and perhaps prove a perpetual Spring of public Misery.—*A Cage*, as the Scripture speaks, *of every unclean Bird*.—The Nursery of Bigotry and Superstition.—An Engine of Persecution, Slavery and Oppression.—A Fountain whose putrid and infectious Streams will overflow the Land, and poison all our Enjoyments. . . .

VII.

Puritan Justice in Transition

No one will ever be able to explain fully why in the spring and summer of 1692 hundreds of people in Massachusetts were accused of witchcraft, or why nineteen were executed for the crime. A few of those convicted were socially marginal figures who may in fact have been trying to practice black magic, but there is no question that at some level the crisis expressed the collective anxiety of an era when the mission of the Puritan fathers seemed irreversibly compromised. Among the accused were a number of prosperous and respected citizens whose involvement in commercial enterprise indicated what the future held for New Englanders. For all the popular passion that undoubtedly was aroused, however, there were no lynchings; where injustice was done, it occurred within the framework of formal legal institutions. In the end, the clergymen of the colony intervened to halt the trials. Led by Increase Mather, president of Harvard College and the man who had negotiated the new royal charter that was so conspicuously offensive to Puritan tradition, they displayed their credentials as members of a learned profession in calling for stricter evidentiary standards. This advice was heeded, as if the clergy constituted an informal court of appeals. The key legal issue thus resolved was the value of "spectral" evidence—testimony concerning the misdeeds not of an actual person, physically present, but of his or her apparition. In their successful argument against convicting on the basis of such testimony, leaders of Massachusetts's ecclesiastical order revealed an appreciation of procedure more rigorous than that of some judges in the mother country, where "spectral" evidence would not necessarily have been excluded. The following selections come from a lengthy treatise that Increase Mather first circulated in manuscript among his fellow ministers in the fall of 1692 and then published the next year. According to Mather, how pervasive was satanic influence in human affairs? What kind of authority did he cite to support his legal conclusions? In practical terms, to what extent did his emphasis on the rights of the innocent pose a challenge to the relentless disciplinary program of the early Puritans?

INCREASE MATHER:
WITCHCRAFT IN MASSACHUSETTS (October 1692)*

The First Case that I am desired to express my Judgment in, is this, Whether it is not Possible for the Devil to impose on the imaginations of Persons Bewitched, and to cause them to Believe that an Innocent, yea that a Pious person does torment them, when the Devil himself doth it; or whether Satan may not appear in the Shape of an Innocent and Pious, as well as of a Nocent and Wicked Person, to Afflict such as suffer by Diabolical Molestations?

The Answer to the Question must be Affirmative.

There are several Scriptures from which we may infer the Possibility of what is Affirmed. . . . In *Rev.* 12.10. the Devil is called the *Accuser of the Brethren.* Such is the malice and impudence of the Devil, as that he does accuse good Men, and that before God, and that not only of such faults as they really are guilty of, but also with such Crimes, as they are altogether free from. He represented the Primitive Christians as the vilest of men, and as if at their Meetings they did commit the most nefandous Villanies that ever were known; and that not only Innocent, but Eminently Pious Persons should thro' the malice of the Devil be accused with the Crime of Witchcraft, is no new thing. Such an Affliction did the Lord see meet

---

* For the complete original text of Mather's argument, which has been much abridged here, see Increase Mather, *Cases of Conscience Concerning Evil Spirits Personating Men; Witchcrafts, Infallible Proofs of Guilt in such as are Accused with that Crime* (Boston, 1693); this is reprinted at the end of Cotton Mather, *The Wonders of the Invisible World* (London, 1862), pp. 221–291.

to exercise the great *Athanasius* with, only the Divine Providence did wonderfully vindicate him from that as well as some other foul Aspersions. The *Waldenses* (altho' the Scriptures call them *Saints, Rev.* 13.7.) have been traduced by Satan and by the World as horrible Witches; so have others in other places, only because they have done extraordinary things by their Prayers. It is by many Authors related, that a City in *France* was molested with a Diabolical *Spectre*, which the people were wont to call *Hugon*; near that place a number of Protestants were wont to meet to serve God, whence the Professors of the true reformed Religion were nic-named *Hugonots*, by the Papists, who designed to render them before the World, as the Servants and Worshippers of that *Daemon*, that went under the name of *Hugon*. And how often have I read in Books written by Jesuits, that *Luther* was a Wizard, and that he did himself confess that he had familiarity with Satan! Most impudent Untruths! Nor are these things to be wondered at, since the Holy Son of God himself was reputed a *Magician*, and one that had Familiarity with the greatest of Devils. . . .

Perhaps some of those whom Satan has represented as committing Witchcrafts, have been tampering with some foolish and wicked Sorceries, tho' not to that degree, which is Criminal and Capital by the Laws both of God and Men; for this Satan may be permitted so to scourge them; or it may be, they have misrepresented and abused others, for which cause the Holy God may justly give Satan leave falsely to represent them.

Have we not known some that have bitterly censured all that have been complained of by bewitched Persons, saying it was impossible they should not be guilty; soon upon which themselves or some near Relations of theirs, have been to the lasting Infamy of their Families, accused after the same manner, and Personated by the Devil? Such tremendous Rebukes on a few, should make all men to be careful how they joyn with Satan in Condemning the Innocent. . . .

Let me further add here; It has very seldom been known, that Satan has Personated innocent Men doing an ill thing, but Providence has found out some way for their Vindication; either they have been able to prove that they were in another place when the Fact was done, or the like. So that perhaps there never was an Instance of any Innocent Person Condemned in any Court of Judicature on Earth, only through Satans deluding and imposing on the Imaginations of Men, when nevertheless, the Witnesses, Juries, and Judges, were all to be excused from blame. . . .

The Truth we affirm is so evident, as that many Learned and Judicious Men have freely subscribed unto it. . . . I have my self known several of whom I ought to think that they are now in Heaven, considering that they were of good Conversation, and reputed Pious by those that had the greatest Intimacy with them, of whom nevertheless, some complained that their Shapes appeared to them, and threatened them. Nor is this answered by saying, we do not know but those Persons might be Witches. We are bound by the Rule of Charity to think otherwise: And they that censure any, meerly because such a sad Affliction as their being falsely represented by Satan has befallen them, do not do as they would be done by. I bless the Lord, it was never the portion allotted to me, nor to any Relation of mine to be thus abused. But no Man knoweth what may happen to him, since *there be just Men unto whom it happeneth according to the Work of the Wicked, Eccles.* 8.14. There is one amongst our selves whom no Man that knows him, can think him to be a Wizzard, whom yet some bewitched Persons complained of, that they are in his Shape tormented: And the Devils have of late accused some eminent Persons.

It is an awful thing which the Lord has done to convince some amongst us of their Error. This then I declare and testifie, that to take away the Life of any one, meerly because a *Spectre* or Devil, in a bewitched or possessed Person does accuse them, will bring the Guilt of innocent Blood on the Land, where such a thing shall be done. Mercy forbid that it should, (and I trust that as it has not it never will be so) in *New-England.* What does such an evidence amount unto more than this: Either such an one did afflict such an one, or the Devil in his likeness, or his Eyes were bewitched. . . .

If the things which have been mentioned are not infallible Proofs of Guilt in the accused Party, it is then Queried, Whether there are any Discoveries of this Crime, which Jurors and Judges may with a safe Conscience proceed upon to the Conviction and Condemnation of the Persons under Suspicion?

Let me here premise Two things,

1. The Evidence in this Crime ought to be as clear as in any other Crimes of a Capital nature. The Word of God does no where intimate, that a less clear Evidence, or that fewer or other Witnesses may be taken as sufficient to convict a Man of Sorcery, which would not be enough to convict him were he charged with another evil worthy of Death. *Numb.* 35.30. If we

may not take the Oath of a distracted Person, or of a possessed Person in a Case of Murder, Theft, Felony of any sort, than neither may we do it in the Case of Witchcraft.

2. Let me premise this also, that there have been ways of trying Witches long used in many Nations, especially in the dark times of Paganism and Popery, which the righteous God never approved of, but which were invented by the Devil, that so innocent Persons might be condemned, and some notorious Witches escape. Yea, many Superstitious and Magical experiments have been used to try Witches by. Of this sort is that of scratching the Witch, or seething the Urine of the Bewitched Person, or making a Witch-cake with that Urine: And that tryal of putting their hands into scalding Water, to see if it will not hurt them: And that of sticking an Awl under the Seat of the suspected Party, yea, and that way of discovering Witches by tying their Hands and Feet, and casting them on the Water, to try whether they will sink or swim. . . .

These things being premised, I answer the Question affirmatively; There are Proofs for the Conviction of Witches which Jurors may with a safe Conscience proceed upon, so as to bring them in guilty. The Scripture which saith, *Thou shalt not suffer a Witch to live*, clearly implies, that some in the World may be known and proved to be Witches: For until they be so, they may and must be suffered to live. Moreover we find in Scripture, that some have been convicted and executed for Witches: For *Saul cut off those that had familiar Spirits, and cast the Wizzards out of the Land*, 1 *Sam.* 28.9. . . .

But then the Enquiry is, What is sufficient Proof? This case has been with great Judgment answered by several Divines of our own. . . . But the Books being now rare to be had, let me express my Concurrence with them in these two particulars.

1. That a free and voluntary Confession of the Crime made by the Person suspected and accused after Examination, is a sufficient Ground of Conviction. Indeed, if Persons are Distracted, or under the Power of *Phrenetick Melancholy*, that alters the Case; but the Jurors that examine them, and their Neighbours that know them, may easily determine that Case; or if Confession be extorted, the Evidence is not so clear and convictive; but if any Persons out of Remorse of Conscience, or from a Touch of God in their Spirits, confess and shew their Deeds, as

the Converted Magicians in *Ephesus* did, *Acts* 19.18, 19,
nothing can be more clear. . . .

2. If two credible Persons shall affirm upon Oath that they have
    seen the party accused speaking such words, or doing such
    things which none but such as have Familiarity with the Devil
    ever did or can do, that's a sufficient Ground for Conviction.

Some are ready to say, that Wizzards are not so unwise as to do
such things in the sight or hearing of others, but it is certain that they
have very often been known to do so. How often have they been seen
by others using Inchantments? Conjuring to raise Storms? And have
been heard calling upon their Familiar Spirits? And have been known
to use Spells and Charms? And to shew in a Glass or in a Shew-stone
persons absent? And to reveal Secrets which could not be discovered
but by the Devil? And have not men been seen to do things which are
above humane Strength, that no man living could do without
Diabolical Assistances? . . . When therefore such like things shall be
testified against the accused Party not by *Spectres* which are Devils in
the Shape of Persons either living or dead, but by real men or
women who may be credited, it is proof enough that such an one has
that Conversation and Correspondence with the Devil, as that he or
she, whoever they be, ought to be exterminated from amongst men.
This notwithstanding I will add; It were better that ten suspected
Witches should escape, than that one innocent Person should be
Condemned. . . . I had rather judge a Witch to be an honest woman,
than judge an honest woman as a Witch. The Word of God directs
men not to proceed to the execution of the most capital offenders,
until such time as upon searching diligently, the matter is *found to be
a Truth, and the thing certain, Deut.* 13.14, 15.

VIII.

The Case For Separation

*During the 1740s and afterward, revivalists in New England used the con-
tractual language of legal discourse at least as often as did advocates of
"liberal" Christianity in advancing the principle of voluntarism against
ecclesiastical authority. The following statement is thought to have been
prepared by a young evangelical clergyman named John Cleaveland in defense
of nineteen "New Lights" who had withdrawn from the Second Church in
Ipswich, Massachusetts. Having grown impatient with the spiritual shortcom-*

ings of their lawfully established minister, Theophilus Pickering, they had
decided without official sanction to form a congregation of their own under
Cleaveland's guidance. Although quite orthodox in his theology, their new
pastor was a man of suitably independent will. A few years earlier, in 1744, he
had been expelled by the president and tutors of Yale College for his support of
lay preachers who were said by the public authorities in Connecticut to have
subverted the standing order of learned clergymen. Cleaveland's theoretical
difficulties in defining exactly what circumstances might dissolve an ecclesiasti-
cal agreement are evident below. According to his argument, would it make
any difference whether the dissidents in question were a tiny fringe group
or a substantial minority? Was it incumbent on them to demonstrate the rea-
sonableness of their views? Cleaveland's later career was less flamboyant,
as he came to appreciate the benefits of clerical office, but in the revolution-
ary era he emerged as a warm proponent of the Patriot cause. Charging the
English government with a breach of "covenant," he would finally exclaim:
"GREAT-BRITAIN adieu!" What might have been the relevance of Separatist
religious logic in a controversy involving political rights and obligations?

JOHN CLEAVELAND: A PLAIN NARRATIVE
(September 1747)*

Before we proceed to the Relation of Facts, we would premise a
few Things, and offer them to the Consideration of the Reader.

1. As all Covenants, so Church-Covenants suppose two Parties,
   each of which have something to perform as a Condition
   dependant on each other.
2. In Church-Covenants, the Privileges and Advantages, such as
   the Word, Sacraments, Discipline agreable to the Gospel, are
   always presupposed, and to be regarded as the Inducements
   with the Person that joins with a Church, who therefore puts
   himself under their Watch and Government, which they
   promise and engage. But if this be neglected by the Church,
   then that Covenant is by them vertually dissolved, and the
   Party injured, in Reason and Justice (if not in Form) at Liberty
   from his Obligation to that Church. Hence,
3. In Case it so happen, thro' the Art and Subtilty of the Pastor
   being himself involved, or the implicit Obedience of a major
   Part of his Church to his Dictates and Designs, or from what
   Cause soever, that the Way to a declared and formal Dissolu-

* From John Cleaveland, *A Plain Narrative Of the Proceedings, which caused The*
Separation of a Number Of aggrieved Brethren . . .(Boston, 1747).

tion of said Covenant . . . is blocked up, and Dismission or Relief not to be obtained in a Way of Order: Then, we say in such a Case, it is lawful, at least excusable, to be sure not answerable to the first Aggressor, for a disappointed and injured Member to seek Relief in a Way extrajudicial, since the main Thing in Religion, *viz.* the Edification of the Person, can't be obtained otherwise. And to this all Forms however useful, must give Way; and hence whatever Injury is thereby done to the Order of the Churches, must in Justice and Equity fall on those that were the Aggressors. . . .

The Case may be thus summed up: A Number of Church Members were offended with the Preaching and Practice of their Pastor, and could get no Redress from him. They then agreable to their Duty and Privilege resulting from their Church-State, laid their Case before the Church. They would do nothing for them, but by their total Negligence, and to say the best of it, their passive Obedience to the Will and Dictates of their Pastor, suffered their offended Brethren to be turned out of the Way of Relief, by any Rule known in our Constitution, thro' Length of Time; which must justly be supposed to be sufficient to dispirit and discourage any meer Man; yea, to produce an utter unfitness for Church Communion and Fellowship together. And not only so, but by their total Negligence to perform this Covenant-Obligation to their Brethren, vertually and in Reason they have dissolved the Obligations on the aggrieved's Part towards them, so that hereby they have left themselves not only without Excuse for their Conduct, but also without Right to complain of any Thing that is done for them by others. Or more shortly thus; We put ourselves under the Bonds of a Covenant with this Church, that we might enjoy the Priviledges of such a State, which they then promised us; but thro' their Neglect or ill Conduct, we could not enjoy those Priviledges; they kept not their Promise to us, so that of Course our Obligations to them, and their Right over us, must be vertually dissolved, and we left at Liberty, to provide for ourselves as before we enter'd into that Covenant. And hence let us put this Question, *what could we have done more*? Or what more in Reason could be expected to be done by us, all Circumstances considered? Which is an Omen of most Evil to these Churches, for a Pastor and Church thus to treat their Members and to pass with Indemnity, or for those Members so treated, to set up for themselves, as we have done?

If it be objected,

Object. That the Articles of Complaint were immaterial and Trifling. We answer,

1. That they were, some of them, of the highest Importance in Religion, both *doctrinal* and *practical*: as not preaching the Doctrines of Grace; his not falling in with, and promoting the Operations of the Holy Spirit upon the Hearts of Men, but treating them and the Subjects of them unseemly, and the like.
2. Our Pastor himself acknowledged they were of Importance, and the Church never pretended the contrary.

Object. If they were of Weight, they were groundless; and were so judged by the Council, that since had the Consideration of them, to whom . . . we submitted our Cause.

To which we say, That we do not take the Argument to lie here: We took them to be real, and that was sufficient. The Question is not now, whether they were groundless or not; but whether (they being thought real by us) the Church ought not to have acted upon them, and advised and admonished the erring Party. . . .

Object. We separated without Order, having no Rule for our Proceedings; and this will encourage others to do the like, and so our Churches are in Danger of being broke up. We Answer,

1. And who was the Cause, and how could we help it, unless we could have contentedly lived without the Ordinances of the Gospel; and would not this have been a paying too great a Compliment to Order? We trust Order is as beautiful in our Eyes, as in the Eyes of other Christians; and that we have taken as much Pains to support it, both before we separated, and since; for this, let what we did for Relief in a Way of Order, and our present Church-State and Behaviour, witness.
2. As to encouraging Separations, and so endangering the Peace of the Churches; we can truly say, that we dislike Separations on trivial and flighty Reasons, as much as any Christians, and would with Humility caution against such, or of taking Example by us, to separate without weighty Reasons. But where Christians are treated by Churches and Pastors, as we have been treated by ours, we have Freedom to say, that we have no great Concern about preserving the outward Peace of such Churches; and we think it highly offensive to God if they do

not separate, since we can't see what Gospel End can be served for Persons to be held down under spiritual Tyranny, in order to support & maintain such a Peace. . . .

3. As to our having no Rule for our Proceeding, we Answer, If we have no particular Rule in the Platform, we have Precedents both in the Word of God, and Church History, to countenance the Thing. As to the Word of God, we find, that it not only justifies us as to the Matter or Foundation-Cause of our Separation, as 2 *Tim.* 3.1–8, 1 *Tim.* 6.3–5. . . . But also as to the manner of it, by the Practice both of the Prophets and Apostles, as *Isai.* 8, 11, 12. . . . As to Church-History, we shall mention only the two great Examples, *viz.* the reformed Churches separating from the romish Church; and the Dissenters from the established Church of *England*; the Lawfulness of which has been sufficiently defended against all Opposers. And altho' we have not equal Reason upon all Accounts with the former, yet we verily think we have with the latter, for what we have done. But whether we have equal Reason with either, yet if we have sufficient Grounds to leave the Church we belonged to, as in Conscience we think we had, and hope we have made sufficiently evident, we may justly plead these Examples for our Justification. . . .

IX.

English Law Summarized

Michael Dalton's popular handbook of English law was often referred to simply as "Dalton's Justice of the Peace," but its complete and exact title was The Countrey Justice, Containing the Practice of the Justices of the Peace out of their Sessions, Gathered for the better helpe of such Justices of Peace as have not been much conversant in the studie of the Lawes of this Realme. *The first edition appeared in 1618, to be followed by numerous others both before and after the author's death around the middle of the century. Although it was not the earliest nor the only influential manual of its kind, colonists in America seemed to find it especially useful. In 1647, for example, the General Court of Massachusetts listed it prominently among a selection of lawbooks ordered from England; and beginning in 1678, the General Assembly of Maryland directed all county courts in the colony to acquire copies of the book. The selections below—a prefatory "Epistle" and a section on "Alehouses"—are taken from an inexpensive sixth edition published in 1643. Dalton himself was a justice of the peace in Cambridge-shire and had studied law at Lincoln's Inn in London, evidently without ever having been admitted to practice as a barrister. England's J. P.s, whom he thought of as his main audience, were usually substantial country gentlemen and frequently could claim at least some formal training in law. How might the author's self-deprecatory introduction have also appealed to colonial officials, in New England and elsewhere? As the discussion of "alehouses" suggests, The Countrey Justice was recognizably a product of the Old World, where indeed popular resistance sometimes made it difficult to enforce the regulations outlined here. How relevant were these "good and profitable Laws" to American circumstances? In particular, would Puritan leaders have wanted to define and tried to solve the problem of public drinking in quite the ways prescribed by Dalton?*

MICHAEL DALTON ON JUSTICES OF THE PEACE (1643)*

EPISTLE (to my Masters of *Lincolnes Inne*):

It may peradventure seeme strange that after so many learned Writers in this kinde, I (a man of so weak parts) should presume to offer to the view of the World, a Work of this nature. Yet my Reasons being considered with indifferent favour, I hope to be excused not onely with you, but with all others that be Lovers of their Country, and seeke the peace thereof. I confess my selfe a long, yet an unprofitable Member of your Honourable Society, but seeing that my calling is to a Country life, and considering that he which is of the meanest condition, and that hath the smallest talent, may not (without just reprehension) retire himself so to his private pleasure, or profit, as that hee should neglect to shew some fruit and token of his love to his Countrey . . ., I have bin the bolder, according to my place, small power and capacity, to offer this my small Mite into the Treasury of my Countrey: this Worke (whatsoever it be) being written first as private Notes for my particular helps in this businesse, wherewith my self and many others are daily imployed, and set on worke, without yeilding any pleasure or profit at all to us, otherwise than for the publike good.

The sweet of like Labours, you my *great Masters* (which I doe most gladly behold) do from time to time reap more fully, rising daily to great Honour and Wealth, through your Wisdomes, Deserts, and great pains; that which remaineth to us Countrey Justicers, (for the most part) is the wearying of our selves, the spending of our time,

---

* Michael Dalton, *The Countrey Justice* . . ., 6th ed. (London, 1643).

wits, and estates, and requited many times not only with much evill will, from or by the meanes of such as wee have in Justice to deal withall, but oftentimes also rather disgraced than countenanced or incouraged by some in higher place. . . .

I acknowledge there be divers other Books in this kinde, more Learned and Methodicall, but withall I observe the businesse of the Justices of Peace, to consist partly in things to be done by them out of their Sessions, (and sometimes privately, and peradventure upon the sudden, without the advice or association of any other) and partly at their Sessions of the Peace. Of things of this last kinde, I purpose not in this Treatise to meddle, for at such publike meetings and assemblies they are far more able to direct themselves; but for the private and sudden helpe of such Justices of peace, who peradventure have not read over the former Writers, and if they have, yet the multiplicity of statutes (whereupon the office and private practice of Justices of Peace doth principally consist) being such, and at every Parliament so altered by expiration, discontinuance, and otherwise, as that it is a worke very hard and laborious, for Gentlemen not conversant in the study of the Laws, although otherwise very industrious, to proceed as by the Commission they ought and are prescribed: upon which consideration, and for their ease principally, I have published this Work. . . . I have therein endeavoured to set down things so plainly, and briefly as I could, with reference to the Statutes abridged, whereby the Reader may the better resolve, and satisfie himselfe what hee ought to doe in every particular almost, that shall come before him. . . .

ALEHOUSES:
The true and principall use of Innes, Alehouses and Victualling houses, is twofold, either for receipt, relief and lodging of wayfaring people traveling from place to place about their necessary businesse, or for the necessary supply of the wants of such poore persons as are not able by greater quantities to make their provision of victuals: and is not meant for entertainment or harbouring of lewd or idle people, to spend or consume their money or time there (as appeareth by the preamble of the Statute made 1 *James cap.* 9). And therefore to prevent the mischiefs, and great disorders hapning daily by the abuses of such houses, his said Majesty of late famous memory, and now our gracious Sovereigne Lord King *Charles*, have graciously bin pleased, that divers good and profitable Laws should be made for the redress thereof, as followeth.

Every keeper of taverne, (keeping also an Inne or victualling in his house) and every Alehouse-keeper, Inne-keeper and Victualler, which shall suffer any Townsman or any handicraftsman, or labourer, working in the same City or Town, to remain and continue drinking in their said house, (except such as shall be invited thither by a Traveller, and during his necessary abode there; and except handicraftsmen, labourers, and workmen, upon the working day, for one hour at dinner, or sojourning or lodging there; or except they be allowed by two Justices of Peace), the said offense being seen by any Justice of Peace within his Limits, or being confessed by the offender, before the Justice of Peace, or being proved before any Justice of Peace, by one witnesse upon oath, every such Taverner, Alehouse-keeper, &c. shall forfeit for every such offence, ten shillings. . . .

If any Taverner (keeping also an Inne, or Victualling in his house) or any Inne-keeper, Alehouse-keeper or Victualler, shall at any time utter or sell within his house, or without, lesse than one full Ale-quart of the best Beer or Ale for one peny, and of the small two quarts for one peny (the said offense being proved before any Justice of Peace, by one witnesse upon oath), then every such Taverner, Inne-keeper, &c. shall forfeit for every such offence twenty shillings. . . .

Every person that shall continue drinking in any Inne or Alehouse, &c. in the Town where he then dwelleth (contrary to the former Statute made 1 *James*), the said offence being seen by any Justice of Peace, or being proved before any Justice of Peace, as aforesaid, such persons shall forfeit for every such offence, three shillings foure pence.

If any other person (wheresoever his or their habitation or abiding be) shall be found by view of any Justice of Peace or by his own confession, or proof of one witnesse, to be tipling in any Inne, Alehouse, or Victualling house, every such person shall be adjudged to be within the said Statutes of 1 *James cap.* 9 & 4 *James cap.* 5, as if he inhabited and dwelt in the City, Town Corporate, or other Town or Village, where the said Inne, Alehouse, or Victualling house is or shall be, where he shall be so found tipling; and he shall incur the like penalty, and the same to be in such sort levied and disposed, as in the said Act is expressed, concerning such as there inhabit. . . .

Every Taverner (keeping also an Inne or Victualling in his house) and every Inne-keeper, Alehouse-keeper, and other Victuallers, which shall suffer any person (wheresoever his dwelling be) to tipple in the said house contrary to the true intent of any of the said former Statutes shall be adjudged within the Statute, 1 *James cap.* 9.

So that now by these Statutes, no person may come to tipple in any such Taverne, or in any Inne, Alehouse, or Victualling house, in the same Town where he dwelleth, nor within two miles thereof, except he be a Traveller; and so Sir *Francis Harvey* delivered it in his charge, at *Cambridge* Summer Assises, *Anno Dom.* 1629. But the Statute 21 *James* & 1 *Charles*, seeme to forbid all tipling in such houses, wheresoever they be, and by whomsoever it be.

Any Justice of Peace in any County (and any Justice of Peace, or other head Officer, in any City or Towne Corporate, within their Limits) shall have power (upon his own view, confession of the party, or proof of one witnesse upon oath) to convict any person of drunkennesse, whereby such persons so convicted shall incur the forfeiture of five shillings for every such offense. . . .

Now for to know a drunken man the better, the Scripture describeth them to stagger and reel to and fro, *Job* 12.25. And so where the same legs which carry a man into the house, cannot bring him out again, it is a sufficient signe of drunkennesse. . . .

X.

Anarchy in Early Virginia

Even at the highest levels of government, public authority in the Chesapeake colonies was unsteady. The tribulations of Governor John Winthrop in Massachusetts were mild compared with those in Virginia of Sir John Harvey, who had received a commission as royal governor from Charles I in 1628 and arrived two years later. An explosive man who lacked political finesse, Harvey was soon quarreling bitterly with his council. Matters came to a head in 1635, as a comical sequence of events culminated in the "thrusting out" of this unfortunate official. In April of that year, local dissidents held a meeting to air their grievances, among them the governor's failure to transmit letters from the General Assembly to the king. Harvey responded to his critics by ordering their arrest, as mutineers, and then summoned his council to pass judgment on them according to martial law. A stormy session ensued, whichever of the two contradictory accounts below should be considered more believable. The first is Harvey's own version of what happened; the second, that of a councilor named Samuel Mathews. Neither says much for the force of law in Virginia, nearly three decades after the colony had been founded. If in fact Harvey referred to himself as "his Majestie's substitute," would this have been a formula that realistically strengthened his position? On what possible grounds might Captain Utie have justified counterarrest of the governor for suspected treason? The immediate aftermath of this episode was that the council named one of its own members as governor and compelled Harvey to return to the mother country. There he managed to rally support, and he eventually made his way back to Virginia. Several councilors were then arrested and sent to England for trial. By intensive lobbying, they not only escaped prosecution but in 1639 finally obtained Harvey's removal from office by order of the Privy Council.

SIR JOHN HARVEY AND THE COUNCIL
OF VIRGINIA (1635)*

Governor Harvey:

Upon the 28 day of Aprill last, which was the time when they were to meet for his Majesties service, Mr. Samuell Mathewes, John Utye, William Farrer, William Pearce, George Minefie and John Pott, all of the councell of Virginia, came armed and brought with them about 50 Musketeers, and besett mee in my owne house, which was the place which I appointed for our meeting. I and Mr. Kemp (his Majesties Secretary there) were then sitting together expecting the councell, when the said mutinous company entered the place, and John Utye in the presence of the rest gave me a very greate and violent stroake upon the shoulder and sayd with a loud voyce, I arrest you for treason; and thereupon Mathewes and the rest of the said company, came all about mee, and layd hould on me, and there held me so as I was not able to stirr from the place, and all of them sayd to me: you must prepare yourself to goe for England, for you must and shall goe, to answer the complaintes that are against you.

Upon this Uproare John Pott (who by the said company was placed at the doore of said house) with his hand gave a signe and immediately the Musketeers, which before that time lay hid, came presently running with their pieces presented towards my house; and when one of my servants saw them coming so hastily towards my house, he asked the said Pott what the said Shott meant. Pott said unto him, Stirr not for your life; and when they were come neare to him, he sayd to the Musketeers: Stay there untill there be use of you; and there upon they retired again. To prepare their way to the

* *Virginia Magazine of History and Biography*, 1 (1894), 416–430; reprinted in Warren M. Billings (ed.) *The Old Dominion in the Seventeenth Century: A Documentary History of Virginia, 1606–1689* (Chapel Hill, N.C., 1975), pp. 251–257.

meeting they caused guards to be sett in all wayes and passages, so that no man could travel or come from place to place, nor had I meanes or power to raise any force to suppress this meeting, they having restrayned me, and sett a guard upon me. . . .

Mathews:

. . . Presently the councell being called together the governor declared it necessary that Martial law should be executed upon the Prisoners; but it was desired they might have legall tryall, soe growing into extreame choler and passion, after many passings and repassings to and fro, he at length sate down in the chayre and with a frowning countenance bid all the councell sit. After a long pause he drew a paper out of his pockett and reading it to himself said to the councell: I am to propound a question unto you; I require every man, in his Majestie's name, to deliver his opinion in writing under his hand, and no man to advise or councell with the other, but to make a direct answer unto this proposition (which is this): What do you think they deserve that have gone about to persuade the people from their obedience to his Majestie's substitute? And to this I doe require you to make your present answer and no man to advise or interrupt with other. And I begin with you Mr. Menefie; who answered: I am but a young Lawyer and dare not upon the suddain deliver my opinion. The governor required that should be his answer under his hand; Mr. Farrar begann to complaine of that strong comand, but the governor cutt off his speech saying in his Majestie's name: I comand you not to speake till your turne. Then myselfe replyed: I conceive this a strange kind of proceeding; instantly in his Majesties name he comanded me silence. I said further there was no Presedent for such a comand, whereupon he gave me leave to speake further, but it was as by a Tyrant (meaning that passage of Richard the third against the Lord Hastings), after which relation the rest of the councell begann to speake and refused that course. Then followed many bitter languages from him, till the sitting ended. The next meeting in a most sterne manner he demanded the reason that wee conceived of the countreye's Petition against him. Mr. Menefee made answer: the chiefest cause was the detayning of the Letters to his Majestie and the Lords. Then he rising in a great rage sayd to Mr. Menefee: and do you say soe? He replied, yes; presently the governor in a fury went and, striking him on the shoulder as hard as I can imagine he could, said: I arrest you of suspicion of Treason to his Majestie. Then

Captain Utie being neare said: and wee the like to you, sir. Whereupon I, seeing him in a rage, tooke him in my armes and said: Sir, there is no harm intended against you save only to acquaint you with the grievances of the Inhabitants and to that end I desire you to sitt downe in youre chayre. And soe I related to him the aforesaid grievances of the colony desiring him that their just complaint might receive some satisfaction, which he altogether denied, soe that sitting ended. . . .

XI.

Competition for Land in New England

The following lawsuit, for trespass, arose out of a land transaction that occurred nearly half a century after the founding of Lynn, Massachusetts. An early Puritan settlement in Essex County, north of Boston, Lynn included much hilly and heavily wooded land, and two swampy marshes. For a time, helped by a grant of extra territory from the central government of the colony, residents of the town had enough usable acreage to satisfy their needs. By 1660, however, the borders of the community had been fixed and its population was increasing significantly, as immigration from the mother country resumed after the Civil War of the 1640s. These circumstances had become more stressful by 1679, when one John Newhall and his nephew of the same name persuaded William Edmonds—an original settler of Lynn—to sell them four unfenced and undeveloped acres adjoining some buildings of their own at a considerable distance from the main inhabited district of the town. Subsequently, as the record shows, the Newhalls cleared timber from this tract, whereupon one Joseph Mansfield went to court claiming the land was actually his. Mansfield's legal action was unsuccessful, which presumably meant that he had to pay the Newhalls' court costs as well as his own, and that the Newhalls' title was guaranteed against anyone else's claim. As usual, there was no account given of the reasoning that led to the verdict. No lawyers participated in the proceedings, and it must be assumed that the jury deliberated without the benefit of strict judicial advice concerning English precedents. What probably were the crucial considerations underlying their decision? The case provides evidence of the informality with which land transactions were conducted in Lynn's formative years and illustrates the process by which landholding in New England was regularized after the middle of the century. It also suggests how that process could be a cause as well as a consequence of disturbing changes in Puritan society. Regardless of their legal vindication, is it possible that in fact the Newhalls were seeking speculative profit from a dubious purchase? If so, can their gain be estimated in monetary terms? To what extent should Mansfield have been consoled by Edmonds's stated intention to renounce payment from the Newhalls? Technically, this litigation took the form of two suits by Joseph Mansfield, Sr., one against the elder John Newhall and one against his nephew; since the defendant in the first prevailed, the second was withdrawn.

IPSWICH QUARTERLY COURT, MASSACHUSETTS: JOSEPH MANSFIELD, SR., V. CORPORAL JOHN NEWHALL AND JOHN NEWHALL II (March 1682)*

John Burrell, sr., aged about forty-seven years, and Joseph Mansfield, jr., aged about twenty-six years, testified that they were desired by Joseph Mansfield, sr., to go to his lot lying by the fresh meadow and there they saw Corp. John Newhall and John, son of Anthony Newhall, cutting and carrying away wood with a team of four oxen, saying this land was theirs. . . .

John Burrell, sr., and Samuel Johnson, aged about thirty-nine years, deposed that they found the stumps of fifty-four trees, large and small, cut and carried away the past winter and appraised the damage at 35 shillings in silver.

William Edmonds certified that he was "ancient" and not able to go to court, and the land in controversy between Joseph Mansfield and the two John Newhalls, all of Lynn, was four acres of land given said Edmonds about forty years ago by Lynn. He sold this to the Newhalls.

Copy of deed, dated 20:11:1679, from William Edmonds of Lynn, tailor, for 30 shillings to John Newhall, sr., of Lynn, son of Thomas Newhall, and John Newhall, 2d, of Lynn, son of Anthony Newhall, four acres, bounded by land once John Leg's on the north, formerly Robert Mansfield's on the south. . . .

Andrew Mansfield, aged about sixty years, and Joseph Mansfield, jr., testified that they went to William Edmonds, who said that he bought the house and house lot of old father Mansfield.

Andrew Mansfield deposed that about forty-three years ago his brother John Mansfield and himself bought of one Manton, so called, a little house, lot and a planting lot, the latter being the lot now in controversy. The next summer their father Robert Mansfield came

---

* Adapted from George F. Dow (ed.), *Records and Files of the Quarterly Courts of Essex County, Massachusetts, 1636–1683* (Salem, Mass., 1911–1921), 8, 253–257.

into the country and they surrendered this estate to him. Manton had bought it of William Edmonds. Two or three years afterward deponent was with his father when Edmonds showed them the boundaries, which were a great white oak and a walnut tree marked, between this land and the lot which was Edward Burcham's.

Record of Robert Mansfield's land, 1649, copied from the town records of Lynn, Mar. 24, 1682, by John Fuller, town clerk: "Two plantting Lotts Lying together . . . , the both Contayning seven Akers moor or Lesse: Lying in the Litle playn that Lyeth norwest of the Fresh marsh; wich marsh Lyeth norwest of the water mill: bounded norwest with the land of Samuell Bennitt: Lately in the Tenure of Edward Burcham. . . ."

Copy of deed, dated June 16, 1652: Robert Mansfield of Lynn, yeoman, for love to his son Joseph Mansfield and for his own good and that of his wife in their old age, all his houses and lands . . ., of which seven acres bounded westerly with the planting lot of or lately in the tenure of Edward Burcham. . . , one half of which houses and lands Joseph was to have at present and the other half at the decease of said Robert, the widow's portion to be considered. . . .

Oliver Purchis certified on Mar. 14, 1681 that ten years ago when he was at the Iron works, formerly called Hammersmith, he was in great need of a tree to make an anvil block and found one that belonged to Joseph Mansfield, sr., who said it was a boundary tree in the line between him and John Newhall, then junior. He said if Newhall consented, he could have it, which he did, and deponent felled the tree in the plain behind the mill street. Stones were laid upon the root to make the boundary mark.

Andrew Mansfield deposed that he laid stones at the root of the boundary tree in the presence of Lieut. Oliver Purchis and Joshua Rhoades, and the new boundary tree was a walnut near the rocks.

"This 19th of March, 1680. Loveing Freinds John Newhall, senior & John Newhall junior, as Concerning the Lot neare to the fresh marsh which was mine, which I have sould you uppon the condicion it was not alienated before, I have furder considered of it, & matters brought to my minde about the Alienateing of it, I would have you desist, & intreat you, not to make any trouble about it. Witnessed: Edward Baker, Andrew Mansfield. Yours in Love: William Edmonds."

Andrew Mansfield testified that Edmonds told him the Newhalls sought him to buy the land in controversy and not he them, and that he was troubled much that he sold it to them and that it had broken his rest many nights. If the Newhalls got the day at law, he would not keep any part of the price but would give it to Joseph Mansfield.

John Newhall, sr.'s bill of cost, 14 shillings. John Newhall, jr.'s bill of cost, 18 shillings.

Verdict for defendants.

XII.
Division of a Planter's Estate

It was customary for gentlemen in the southern colonies to draw up complicated wills that took the needs and interests of various children into account. One example from Virginia is the will of George Washington's father, Augustine, who died unexpectedly in April of 1743, before reaching the age of fifty. On the day before his death, in grave condition, he worked out the terms of the document that follows. There were two surviving sons by a first marriage, Lawrence and Augustine, Jr., in order of age; since Augustine, Sr., had not remained a widower for long, there were four more surviving sons and one daughter by his second marriage. George, the first-born of these, was eleven when his father died. A planter with aggressive business instincts, Augustine Washington owned different tracts of land totaling upward of ten thousand acres. Predictably, the larger part of this estate went to Lawrence; but the other sons were not neglected, and elaborate arrangements were made to redivide the family's property in certain specified circumstances. What might explain the almost obsessive concern of Augustine, Sr., to anticipate so many contingencies? Although the father was not wealthy enough to set up each son in the grand style of a first-class planter, none would be left without a moderate inheritance. The widow and daughter were also provided for, according to alternative formulas typical of the time and place. Does this will indicate that Augustine Washington was sentimentally attached to particular lands? To what extent does he appear to have distributed his property with an eye toward maintaining a quasi-aristocratic sense of family pride and identity? Note that the text is lacking in any personal religious confession of the kind that had introduced the wills of Augustine's father and grandfather.

WILL OF AUGUSTINE WASHINGTON (April 11, 1743)*

In the name of God Amen.

I Augustine Washington of the County of King George, Gentleman: being sick and weak but of Perfect and Disposing Sence and

---

* From Stanislaus Murray Hamilton (ed.), *Letters to Washington and Accompanying Papers*, 5 vols. (Boston, 1898–1902), 3, 392–397.

Memory do make my Last will and Testament in Manner following here by Revoking all former will or wills whatsoever by me hertofore made.

I give unto my Son Lawrence Washington & his Heirs for ever All that Plantation and Tract of Land at Hunting Creek in the County of Prince William Containing by Estimation Two Thousand five Hundred Acres with the water mill Adjoining thereto or Lying Near the same, and all the Slaves Cattle and Stocks of all Kinds whatsoever & all the Houshold Furniture Whatsoever now in and upon or which have been Commonly Poses'd by my said son together with the Said Plantation Tract of Land and mill.

I give Unto my son Augustine Washington and his Heirs for Ever all my Lands in the County of Westmorland Except such only as are herein after otherwise Disposed of. Together with Twenty five Head of Cattle, forty Hogs and Twenty Sheep and a Negro Man named Frank besides those Negros formerly Given him by his Mother.

I give unto my said son Augustine three Young Working Slaves to be purchased for him out of the first Profits of the Iron Works after my Decease.

I give Unto my son George Washington and his Heirs the Land I now Live on which I Purchased of the Executrix of Mr. William Strother Deceased, and one Moiety of my Land Lying on Deep Run and [blank] Negro Slaves.

I give Unto my son Samuel Washington & his Heirs my Land at Chotank in the County of Stafford Containing about Six Hundred Acres and Also the other Moiety of my Tract of Land Lying on Deep Run.

I give unto my Son John Washington and his Heirs my Land at the Head of Maddox in the County of Westmorland Containing About Seven Hundred Acres.

I give unto my Son Charles Washington and his Heirs the Land I Purchased of my son Lawrence Washington (whereon Thomas Lewis now Lives) Adjoyning to my said son Lawrence's Land Above Devised. I also give Unto my said son Charles and his Heirs the Land I Purchased of Gabril Adams, in the County of Prince William, Containing about Seven Hundred Acres.

It is my will and Desire that all the Rest of my Negros not herein Particularly Devised may be Equally Divided between my Wife and my three sons Samuel John & Charles and that Ned Jack Bob Sue & Lucy may be Included in my Wifes part, which part of my said Wifes after her Decease I Desire may be Equally Divided between my sons George Samuel John & Charles. . . .

I give and Bequeath Unto my said Wife and four sons George Samuel John & Charles all the Rest of my Personall Estate to be Equally Divided Between them which is not Particularly Bequeath'd By this my Will. And it is my Will & Desire that my said four Sons Estates may be Kept in my Wifes hands untill they Respectively Attain the Age of Twenty one years, in Case my Said Wife Continues so Long Unmarried, but in Case She Should happen to marry before that time I desire it may be In the power of my Executors to oblige her Husband from time to time as they shall think proper to give Security for the performance of this my Last will in paying & Delivering my said four sons their Estates Respectively as they come of age or on failure to give such Security to take my said sons & their Estates out of the Custody & Tuition of my said wife & her Husband.

I give and Bequeath unto my said wife the Crops made at Bridge Creek Chotank and Rappahannock quarters at the time of my Decease for the Suport of her Self and her Children & I Desire my Wife may Have the Liberty of working my Land at Bridge Creek quarter for the term of five Years Next after my Decease. . . .

I give to my son Lawrence Washington and the Heirs of his Body Lawfully Begotten for Ever that Tract of land I purchased of Mr. James How Adjoyning to the said Lawrence Washingtons Land on Mattox in the County of Westmorland, which I give him in lieu of the Land my Said son bought for me in Prince William County of Spence & Harrison, & for want of such Heirs then I give & devise the Land to my Son Augustine and his Heirs for Ever.

I give to my said son Lawrence all the Right title & Interest I have to in or out of the Iron Works in which I am concernd in Virginia and Maryland, Provided that he do & shall out of the profits Raised thereby Purchase for my son Augustine three young Working Slaves as have herein Before been Directed and Also pay my Daughter Betty when she Arives to the age of Eighteen Years the sum of four Hundred pounds, which Right Title and Interest on the Condition Aforesaid I give to my said son Lawrence and his Heirs for Ever.

I give Unto my said daughter Betty a Negro Child named Mary, Daughter to Sue, & Another named Betty, daughter to Judy.

It is my will & desire that my sons Lawrence and Augustine do pay out of the Respective Estate Devised to them one half or Moiety of the Debts I justly owe & for that purpose I give and bequeath to my two sons one half of the Debts due and owing to me.

Forasmuch as my Severall Children in this my Will Mentioned being by Severall Venters Cannot Inherit from one Another, in Order to make proper provission against their Dying Without Issue It is my will & Desire that in Case my Son Lawrence Should die without Heirs of his Body Lawfully Begotten that then the Land & mill Given him by this my Will Lying in the County of Prince William Shall go and Remain to my son George & his Heirs, but In Case my son Augustine should Chose to have the Said Land Rather than the Land he holds in Mattox Either by this will or any Settlement then I give and Desire the Said Lands in Prince William to my Said Son Augustine and his Heirs on his Conveying the Said Lands in Mattox to my said son George and his Heirs, and in Case my said son Augustine Shall happen to dye without Issue of his Body Lawfully Begotten then I Give and Bequeath all the said Lands by him held in Mattox to my said son George and his Heirs, and if both my sons Lawrence and Augustine should happen to dye without Issue of their Severall Bodys Begotten then my Will and Desire is that my son George and his Heirs may have his and their Choice to have Either the Lands of my Son Lawrence or the Lands of my Son Augustine to hold to him and his Heirs, and the Lands of such of my said sons Lawrence or Augustine as Shall not be so chosen by my son George or his Heirs Shall go to and Be Equally Divided among my Sons Samuel John & Charles and their Heirs Share & Share Alike, and in Case my son George by the Death of both or Either of my Sons Lawrence and Augustine Should According to this my Intention come to Be posses'd of either of their Lands then my will and Desire is that the Lands hereby Devis'd to my said son George and his Heirs Shall Go Over and be Equally Divided Between my sons Samuel & John and their Heirs Share & Share Alike, and in Case all my Children by my present Wife Should happen to dye without Issue of their Bodys Then my will and Desire is that all the Lands by this my will Devised to any of my said Children should go to my sons Augustine & Lawrence if Living and to their Heirs, and if one of them Should be Dead without Issue then to the Survivor and his Heirs. But my True Meaning is that Each of my Children by my Present Wife may have their Lands in fee Simple Upon the Contingency of their Arriving at full Age or Leaving Heirs of their Bodys Lawfully Begotten, or on their dying Under Age and without Lawfull Issue then their Severall parts to

Desend from one to a Nother According to their Course of Desents, and the Remainder of any of their Land in this Claws mentioned to my sons Lawrence & Augustine or the Survivor of them is only Upon the Contingency of all my Said Children by my present wife dying under Age & without Issue Leaving my sons Lawrence and Augustine or Either of them.

Lastly I constitute and Appoint my son Lawrence Washington and my good Friends Danniel McCarty and Nathaniel Chapman, Gentlemen, Executors of this my Last will and Testament. In Witness Whereof I have hereunto sett my Hand & Seal. . . .

XIII.
The Heavy Hand of the Privy Council

The case of Winthrop v. Lechmere *originated in the claim of a latter-day John Winthrop, whose family tree included not only Massachusetts's first governor but two governors of Connecticut. In 1717, Winthrop's father had died intestate—that is, without leaving a will; as the eldest son, John insisted that he was entitled to inherit all real estate according to the English rule of primogeniture. (See the Essay, pp. 42–43.) After an adverse decision in Connecticut's Court of Probate, he ignored his right of appeal to the colonial Court of Assistants and proceeded directly to the Privy Council. Its order favoring Winthrop, issued in 1728 after hearings in which Connecticut was not officially represented, came as a blow to political leaders struggling to defend the terms of the colony's self-governing charter. Governor Joseph Talcott, elected locally, therefore sent the following instructions to Jonathan Belcher, one of the colony's designated agents in London. The constitutional argument advanced by Talcott relied on a theory of "conquest" that was going out of fashion in the eighteenth century. (See the Essay, p. 17.) What might have led the governor to adopt this line of reasoning, which justified Connecticut's independence only until such time as the mother country should see fit to intervene forthrightly? To what extent did Talcott dilute the special heritage of his region in order to frame a statement that would refer to imperial as well as colonial interests? Although unsympathetic to the colony's broader constitutional claims, the Privy Council backed off from its new policy toward New England's traditional rules of inheritance. But* Winthrop v. Lechmere *was a warning of what might happen to the customary law of the colonies in an era of intensified imperial surveillance.*

JOSEPH TALCOTT TO JONATHAN BELCHER
(December 19, 1728)*

Sir: After you have presented an Address to their Majesties, and acquainted yourself with the state of our affairs, and shall have obtain'd a reconsideration of that which affects us in the Determination of his Majesty in Council, namely, the vacating our law concerning Intestate Estates, the arguments which we have prepared for you are as follows:

It has been the uninterrupted practice of the people settled within the limits of Connecticut to make laws to govern themselves by, which now runs well nigh to an hundred years, as appears by all our ancient monuments and records. The body of which laws have been twice by order of the Lords of Trade laid before his Majesties predecessors and no exception taken against them, notwithstanding the first law in the book does declare that the people in the Colony shall be govern'd by the laws of this Colony, and where no law is provided, by the law of God, agreeable to the Resolve of the late Queen Ann in Council on a case from Jamaica, wherein it was Resolved, That in an uninhabited Country, settled by the King's Subjects, the laws of the nation should be their laws; but in a conquered Country, the laws of equity and nations, till the conqueror has declar'd his laws. And our Royal Charter shows this Colony to be in part conquered, and the rest not uninhabited. And of all the laws that have ever been made in this Colony, on all the Complaints that have ever heretofore been, this Corporation have never been required or directed to correct more than one of them, and that only in one article, namely, so far as it concern'd Quakers, which part of the said law was repeal'd accordingly by our General Assembly, and an exception ever makes the rule strong. And the way by which the Kings of Great Britain have established law to this Colony is by the Acts of this Corporation pursuant to the Charter. A further sanction of this authority has also been given by the affirmation of judgments here given by and according to these laws. If such an authority has been used for the space of an hundred years, and from the first date without interruption, 'tis humbly prayed it may not now be disallowed.

---

* Mary Kingsbury Talcott (ed.), *The Talcott Papers: Correspondence and Documents*, 2 vols. (Hartford, Conn., 1892–1896), 1, 143–158.

Dividing Intestate Estates among all a man's children has been the universal custom in this Colony from the beginning of its plantation, which is beyond the memory of man, as may be seen by the copies of Record, ancient and modern.

That this is a reasonable custom will appear if it be considered that in the first settlement of the Country lands were the least valuable part of men's estates, and so should be much rather subject to a division than chattels. Land was plenty and chattels scarce; so that without a division of the lands as well as chattels, very little could be assigned to any except the eldest son. And the land itself must have remained unoccupy'd, if it had not been divided. It was esteem'd much in favour of creditors when they were not obliged to take lands in satisfaction of their debts, and it remains so to this time. It was inhabitants and not land that was wanting; yea, it was common in dividing lands among the inhabitants to oblige them to hold the land they had once accepted, that they might bear the burthen of Taxes and fencing. And much of our lands remain yet unsubdued, and must continue so without the assistance of the younger sons, which in reason can't be expected if they have no part of the inheritance; for in this poor country, if the landlord lives, the tenant starves; few estates here will let for little more than for maintaining fences and paying taxes. By this custom of dividing inheritances, all were supply'd with land to work upon, the land as well occupy'd as the number of hands would admit of, the people universally imploy'd in husbandry; thereby considerable quantities of provision are rais'd, and from our stores the trading part of the Massachusetts and Rhoad Island are supply'd, the fishermen are subsisted, and most of the sugars in the West Indies are put up in casks made of our staves. By this means our predecessors were enabled to furnish themselves with almost all their cloathing, nails and most other necessaries from their neighbours at Boston, (who transport them from Great Britain) and so we do this day. By means of this custom, his Majesties Subjects are here increas'd, the younger brethren do not depart from us, but others are rather encouraged to settle among us, and it's manifest that New England does populate faster than the Colonies where the land descends according to the rules of the common law. And such measures as will furnish the best infantry do most prepare for the defence of a people settled in their enemies country.

That this law should be favour'd and allow'd of, appears from the inconveniencies that will follow upon its being vacated.

In that, all the settlements of lands left intestate and all the alienations under such settlements will be overthrown thereby, by which means almost every man in the Colony will be turn'd out of his house and land, or some of his improvements. We are now arrived to the third, fourth and fifth generation, and many families who proceeded from one stock, are branch'd into twenty, forty, and it may be some sixty or more descendants, and by their sweat and toil, and the labors of their fathers and grandfathers, the lands they now possess were reduced from a mere chaos, and a thing of little or no value, to be sufficient to subsist a numerous offspring. And now to be turn'd out of all by the eldest descendants from our great-grand-fathers, who had nothing but a thing of nought in it, will be so far from the rules of equity and justice, that we presume the common law will never put it upon us. Quarrels and lawsuits will abound, when matters of fact shall be judg'd of by rules unknown to the transactors of them. Most of our lands will lie unoccupy'd. Multitudes will be undone and beggar'd, when their lands are taken from them, not being brought up in manufactures, but husbandry only. . . .

The just designs and dependence of the deceased, to have their children provided for, after their decease, by this law, will be frustrated; and by plentiful evidence it might be made to appear that many, and not of the least estate, have declared they would not make any will, because the law of the country was agreeable to their minds, and so died without making any other, but resigning what they had to the disposal of the said law.

And the further inconveniencies on others, which the vacating this law will have a tendency to, are too manifest. The abatement of our husbandry will abate the trade of the neighbouring Provinces, the fishery, &c, who have a considerable dependence on our husbandry, and the abatement of the fishery will affect the British Trade.

The increase of his Majesties Subjects in this Colony will be diminished. And as to the younger generation, necessity will require their being brought up to trades, or leave their country, and the promoting manufactures here will not be favour'd in Great Britain. . . .

And seeing that above thirty years past, at the desire of their

Lordships of the Board of Trade, our late Governor Winthrop sent our laws, and that among them was sent to their Lordships the law making Intestate Estates divideable among the children, the eldest son having a double portion, from that day to this we never heard that our laws were faulted, excepting only in the forementioned article about the Quakers, and now in this case of Mr. Winthropp's. And truly we had the vanity to think, (if it must be so accounted) that we were very safe, since their Lordships (who acted, as they said, by an express Order from his then Majesty King William) found no fault in our said law, and we copy'd after the Massachusetts, which could not be law if disapprov'd of by his Majesty, and specially since our Colony is newer than theirs, and therefore the reason enforcing their law is here stronger. . . .

Whereupon it's humbly prayed that our law concerning Intestate Estates, declared to be void in the case between Mr. Winthropp and Mr. Lechmere, in which we had no opportunity to set that matter in its just light, may be allow'd and approv'd. . . .

XIV.

Lawyers Against Pettifoggers

As in the mother country, public disparagement of lawyers in the colonies often reflected the hostility of leading practitioners toward lesser figures in the profession. Such was the way of New York's William Livingston, generally acknowledged to be the intellectual leader of the "triumvirate" that tried to block Anglican plans for King's College. (See pp. 85–86.) Among Livingston's early publications was The Art of Pleading, In Imitation of Part of Horace's Art of Poetry *(1751), an anonymous effort from which the following mock address and verses have been taken. Although his satire derived from English literary conventions, the targets of its criticism were local. What might have been Livingston's motives in choosing so stylized a mode of expression? Whom could it have impressed, and with what advantage to the author? Is there a pattern of resentment revealed here, alongside the habitual superciliousness of a well-educated young gentleman? Later, as his legal business grew, Livingston had some success promoting higher professional standards for the New York bar. His own office offered each clerk a course of study that included such subjects as history and rhetoric, to "contribute their part to the perfecting a Scholar." And in 1770, he was a prime mover in founding a kind of legal seminar known as "The Moot," in imitation of such a forum at Gray's Inn, London. Little wonder, then, that one New Yorker at the time—though no admirer of professionalized lawyers—had to concede that few other men in the province could lay claim to a "literature."*

WILLIAM LIVINGSTON: THE ART OF PLEADING (1751)*

To all the Pettifoggers in New York:

Gentlemen,

. . . Moving in an elevated Station, and enroll'd in one of the most honourable Professions, yours is the wondrous Talent of being familiar with the Vulgar, with I know not what of a magnificent Condescention; and of mingling with the *Porter* and the *Tar*, with a kind of lowly rustic Majesty. So great, in fine, are your personal Excellencies, that they are only transcended by your publick Vertues, and your inimitable and unintermitted Services to your Country. For, instead of rendering your Profession wholly venal, how numerous and diffusive are the kind of Offices you dispense amongst your fellow Creatures, for Rewards, by more than half, inadequate to your indefatigable Labours! While the other Gentlemen of the *Robe* practise with the selfish View to private Advantage, your disinterested Bosoms swell with a glorious *Philanthropy*; and instead of the rigourous Demand of a *Quantum Meruit* for your Trouble, you frequently toil for the unlucrative Consideration of natural Love and Affection. Nor content to wait the dilatory Process of Law, you often accelerate your Client's Remedy, by acting in the double Capacity, of Attorney, and Bailiff. At other Times, (such is your immensurable Generosity) you compromise the Controversy, by the voluntary Accord of the Litigants. Thus to the honour'd Character of *Lawyers*, you superadd the more exalted Title of *Peace-makers*; and besides your *Freehold Inheritances* on Earth, piously secure the Kingdom of Heaven in *Reversion*. Nor can I forbear remarking, that some of you, to your immortal Honour, not even satisfied with recovering a Client's Demand without his Trouble, have generously endeavour'd to save him the Trouble of receiving it from you.

Thus conscious of your superior Utility to the City, justly might some of you enter into a Confederacy to suppress the rising Generation of Attornies, and laudably endeavour to perplex and ruin their Practice, by preventing or delaying the Execution of their Process. . . .

---

* Excerpted from William Livingston, *The Art of Pleading, In Imitation of Horace's Art of Poetry* (New York, 1751).

Suppose a Limner figur'd in a Piece,
A Horse's Body with a human Face:
Above a Virgin, beautiful and hale,
But shap'd beneath into a Fish's Tail;
At last, in varied Plumage drest the Whole,
Wou'd you not laugh, and brand him a Fool?
Just so th' unletter'd Blockheads of the *Robe*,
(Than whom no greater Monsters on the Globe)
Their Wire-drawn, incoherent, Jargon spin,
Or lug a Point by Head and Shoulders in.

Some Lawyers at the op'ning of a Cause,
Set out with mighty Pomp to gain Applause,
But finding instantly their Want of Skill,
With *Hums* and *Haws*, their Declamations fill.

Some of the Robe commit the grossest Fault,
When aiming to be brief, they cloud a Thought:
Or striving to be florid, are undone,
And talk but more elaborately wrong.

Thus want of Learning, join'd with want of Sense,
Is the most certain Source of Impudence.

Rather than have the Name of such a Quack,
I'd take the Pedlar's Burden on my Back,
And range content, the spacious Province round,
Tho' yearly gaining less than Twenty Pound.
For what altho' thou can'st sum up in *Debt*,
With general Eulogy, and great Eclat;
Will that small Art enable thee to draw,
A solemner *Argument* on *Points in Law*?

Before thou tak'st the venerable Gown,
To pause a while, contented, set thee down;
Weigh all thy Strength, thy Genius well peruse,

And then as Nature dictates, boldly chuse.
If she directs to *Law*, thine Ear incline,
And thou at Law, undoubtedly will shine,
Nor be perplex'd concerning Eloquence,
Language will flow, when thou hast Law and Sense.
But if reluctant to the fair Employ,
She points to some factitious Mystery;
Avoid, avoid, the inextricable Snare,
Nor madly venture to approach the Bar;
But instant clipping vain Ambition's wing,
Turn *Carman*, *Cobler*, *Fiddler*, any Thing.

XV.

The Ambiguities of Resistance

Unexpectedly, in Boston and other colonial port towns, demonstrations against the Stamp Act of 1765 had triggered violent crowd activity. Repeal the next year calmed the political scene; but then in 1767, "Champagne Charlie" Townshend persuaded Parliament to impose duties on glass, lead, paints, paper, and tea imported by the colonies from the mother country. Early in December, the first of John Dickinson's "Letters from a Farmer in Pennsylvania, to the Inhabitants of the British Colonies" appeared anonymously in a Philadelphia newspaper. This and the eleven that succeeded it were widely reprinted. Most or all of the letters were published in a total of nineteen colonial weeklies; there were also seven American pamphlet editions. According to one calculation, Dickinson's message reached well over one-third of the literate political audience in British North America. At the outset, few people knew the identity of the "farmer." Dickinson was a prosperous lawyer in his middle thirties who had been trained both in a Philadelphia office and at the Middle Temple, London. What rhetorical advantage might he have hoped to gain by adopting the persona of a learned landowner? Because the author was eloquent on the need for vigilant defense of colonial liberties, and withering in his criticism of the argument that "external" taxes were acceptable, such radicals as Sam Adams were able to make effective use of the "Farmer's Letters." In the end, however, Dickinson declined to sign the Declaration of Independence. Do the following excerpts suggest why? To what extent do they reflect the outlook of a professionalized colonial lawyer? Dickinson's decision in 1776 damaged his subsequent political career, despite the services he rendered to the American cause during the war.

JOHN DICKINSON'S LETTERS FROM
A FARMER (1767–1768)*

My Dear Countrymen,

I am a FARMER, settled after a variety of fortunes, near the banks, of the river *Delaware*, in the province of *Pennsylvania*. I received a liberal education, and have been engaged in the busy scenes of life: But am now convinced, that a man may be as happy without bustle, as with it. My farm is small, my servants are few, and good; I have a little money at interest; I wish for no more. My employment in my own affairs is easy; and with a contented grateful mind, I am compleating the number of days allotted to me by divine goodness.

Being master of my time, I spend a good deal of it in a library, which I think the most valuable part of my small estate; and being acquainted with two or three gentlemen of abilities and learning, who honour me with their friendship, I believe I have acquired a greater share of knowledge in history, and the laws and constitution of my country, than is generally attained by men of my class, many of them not being so fortunate as I have been in the opportunities of getting information.

From infancy I was taught to love humanity and liberty. Inquiry and experience have since confirmed my reverence for the lessons then given me, by convincing me more fully of their truth and excellence. Benevolence towards mankind excites wishes for their welfare, and such wishes endear the means of fulfilling them. Those can be found in liberty alone, and therefore her sacred cause ought to be espoused by every man, on every occasion, to the utmost of his power. As a charitable but poor person does not withhold his *mite*, because he cannot relieve *all* the distresses of the miserable, so let not any honest man suppress his sentiments concerning freedom, however small their influence is likely to be. . . .

The meaning of these letters is, to convince the people of these colonies, that they are at this moment exposed to the most imminent dangers; and to persuade them immediately, vigourously, and unanimously, to exert themselves, in the most firm, but most peaceable manner for obtaining relief.

The cause of liberty is a cause of too much dignity, to be sullied by turbulence and tumult. It ought to be maintained in a manner

* Adapted from John Dickinson, *Letters from a Farmer in Pennsylvania* . . ., ed. R. T. H. Halsey (New York, 1903), Letters 1, 3, & 5.

suitable to her nature. Those who engage in it, should breathe a sedate, yet fervent spirit, animating them to actions of prudence, justice, modesty, bravery, humanity, and magnanimity. . . .

I hope, my dear countrymen, that you will in every colony be upon your guard against those who may at any time endeavour to stir you up, under pretences of patriotism, to any measures disrespectful to our sovereign and our mother country. Hot, rash, disorderly proceedings, injure the reputation of a people as to wisdom, valour and virtue, without procuring them the least benefit. I pray God, that he may be pleased to inspire you and your posterity to the latest ages with that spirit, of which I have an idea, but find a difficulty to express: to express in the best manner I can, I mean a spirit that shall so guide you, that it will be impossible to determine, whether an *American*'s character is most distinguishable for his loyalty to his sovereign, his duty to his mother country, his love of freedom, or his affection for his native soil.

Every government, at some time or other, falls into wrong measures; these may proceed from mistake or passion. But every such measure does not dissolve the obligation between the governors and the governed; the mistake may be corrected; the passion may pass over.

It is the duty of the governed, to endeavour to rectify the mistake, and appease the passion. They have not at first any other right, than to represent their grievances, and to pray for redress, unless an emergency is so pressing, as not to allow time for receiving an answer to their applications, which rarely happens. If their applications are disregarded, then that kind of opposition becomes justifiable, which can be made without breaking the laws, or disturbing the public peace. This consists in the prevention of the oppressors reaping advantage from their oppressions, and not in their punishment. For experience may teach them what reason did not; and harsh methods, cannot be proper, till milder ones have failed.

If at length it becomes undoubted, that an inveterate resolution is formed to annihilate the liberties of the governed, the English history affords frequent examples of resistance by force. What particular circumstances will in any future case justify such resistance, can never be ascertained till they happen. Perhaps it may be allowable to say, generally, that it never can be justifiable, until the people are FULLY CONVINCED, that any further submission will be destructive to their happiness.

When the appeal is made to the sword, highly probable it is, that the punishment will exceed the offence; and the calamities attending on war out weigh those preceding it. These considerations of justice and prudence, will always have great influence with good and wise men. . . .

We cannot act with too much caution in our disputes. Anger produces anger; and differences that might be accommodated by kind and respectful behaviour, may by imprudence be changed to an incurable rage.

In quarrels between countries, as well as in those between individuals, when they have risen to a certain heighth, the first cause of dissention is no longer remembred, the minds of the parties being wholly engaged in recollecting and resenting the mutual expressions of their dislike. When feuds have reached that fatal point, all considerations of reason and equity vanish; and a blind fury governs, or rather confounds all things. A people no longer regards their interest, but the gratification of their wrath.

Wise and good men in vain oppose the storm, and may think themselves fortunate, if, endeavouring to preserve their ungrateful fellow citizens, they do not ruin themselves. Their prudence will be called baseness; their moderation, guilt; and if their virtue does not lead them to destruction, as that of many other great and excellent persons has done, they may survive, to receive from their expiring country, the mournful glory of her acknowledgment, that their councils, if regarded, would have saved her. . . .

How many British authors have remonstrated that the present wealth, power and glory of their country are founded on these colonies? As constantly as streams tend to the ocean, have they been pouring the fruits of all their labours into their mother's lap. Good Heaven! And shall a total oblivion of former tendernesses and blessings be spread over the minds of a wise people, by the sordid acts of intriguing men, who covering their selfish projects under pretences of public good, first enrage their countrymen into a frenzy of passion, and then advance their own influence and interest, by gratifying that passion, which they themselves have basely excited?

Hitherto Great-Britain has been contented with her prosperity. Moderation has been the rule of her conduct. But now a generous and humane people that so often has protected the liberty of strangers, is inflamed into an attempt to tear a privilege from her own children, which, if executed, must in their opinion, sink them into slaves. And for what? For a pernicious power, not necessary to her, as her own experience may convince her, but horribly dreadful and detestable to them.

It seems extremely probable, that when cool, dispassionate posterity shall consider the affectionate intercourse, the reciprocal benefits, and the unsuspecting confidence, that have subsisted between these colonists and their parent country, for such a length of time, they will execrate with the bitterest curses the infamous memory of those men, whose pestilential ambition, unnecessarily, wantonly, first opened the sources of civil discord, between them; first turned their love into jealousy; and first taught these provinces, filled with grief and anxiety, to enquire,

> *"Mens ubi materna est?"*
> Where is maternal affection?

A FARMER.

XVI.
Insurrection in the Countryside

At the conclusion of the Seven Years' War, Monmouth County in East Jersey was a debt-ridden rural area suffering from the economic liabilities of poor soil and dense forest. Grassroots anger boiled over in the late 1760s. As the first of the statements below indicates, complaints focused on the legal profession, which was blamed not only for high fees and court costs but also for provincial statutes that made it easier for creditors to recover what was owed them. What additionally was signified by the distinctive language used in this document? In July of 1769, a mob tried to bar lawyers from entering the county court of common pleas; what happened is described in the second statement. Early in 1770, a full-scale insurrection forced officials to suspend the county court of quarter sessions for its January term. The rioting spread to nearby Essex County, prompting Governor William Franklin—Benjamin's Tory son—to deplore the "general Licentiousness of the Times." He dismissed the issue of court costs as a mere "Pretence," saying that the disturbances had been caused by "the Unwillingness of some, and the Inability of others, to pay their just Debts." For its part, the provincial Assembly made few concessions to the insurgents, so their cause ultimately failed. Despite a local record of popular resistance to taxation by the mother country, why might some inhabitants of this area have later been reluctant to support the American side in the War of Independence?

GRIEVANCES OF MONMOUTH COUNTY, NEW JERSEY (1769)*

My dear Countrymen:

Permit me to declare to you my deep Concern for you and myself, in regard to the present deplorable and afflictive Times, which brings to my Mind the past heavy Burthens we have struggled through; it is but a few Years ago, when we were burthened with a long, tedious and expensive War, which drained our Country in a great Measure, of both Men and Money; but as it was in Defence of our Rights and Liberties, we cheerfully struggled through the same.

Secondly, we were burthened with a most Destructive, alarming, and unconstitutional Act of Parliament, (*to wit* the Stamp Act) and that from our Mother Country, the Thoughts of which alarmed every considerate Breast, from the highest to the lowest Rank of People, every one calling out for Liberty and Property. The Consequence of which, was, that by a steady, firm and undaunted Resolution, in Opposition to so unconstitutional an Act, we as Freemen held our Right to Freedom, and boldly withstood the Threats, and at length were heard by our Mother, our Grievance redressed, and we restored to our former Liberties.

Thirdly, We having by our Good Resolutions turned out the wounding and devouring Serpent, and then setting ourselves down easy, and not keeping out a resolute Watch, have let in Serpents seven Times more devouring than the first (*to wit* L—yrs), who in their daily Practice are as Private Leaches, sucking out our very Hearts Blood. Our public Houses are papered with Sheriff's Advertisements, and we daily hear our Neighbour's Lands and Goods sold for not much more than one Fourth Part of the Value, whereby the Man is ruined, and his Family turned out of Doors, and his whole Estate not amounting to more than Lawyer's and Sheriff's Fees, while the Creditor is wanting his Money; and in the next Place the Debtor is hurried to Gaol, there to starve and suffer, while his Family are in the like Condition at home. The Consideration of which makes me cry out to you my Countrymen, Rouse, Rouse! and shake off your drowsy and stupid Delays; open your Eyes, and you will see the ruinous State of your Country, and say with David of old, that the Hand that deliver'd us out of the Paw of the Lyon and the Bear, shall he not deliver us out of the Hands of the uncircumcised L—yrs? We all of us complain of the Hardness of the Times, but not one of us offers to forward any Means to shake off the Burthen. David would never have slain the uncircumcised Philistine, had

---

* Derived from an anonymous pamphlet entitled *Liberty and Property, Without Oppression* (n.p., 1769).

he not used Means for that Purpose; neither shall we ever overcome the ungrateful L—yrs, if we do not bestir ourselves. Consider the daily Practice of those Gentlemen of the Law, as they Stile themselves: what extravagant Bills of Cost are made, and Escapes brought against Sheriffs, when they already have got the Man's whole Estate? We are free People, & shall we be brought to Slavery, and that by a Set of People brought up among us, who are living upon the Ruins of the Poor, and will hardly look at a common Man, when they meet him, unless they can persuade him to have an Action brought against one or another of his Neighbours? We were deemed a People of good Courage and undaunted Resolution, when we withstood the Stamp-Act; and shall we now give away our all to this unconscionable Set of L—yrs? No, but let us with the same manly Spirit withstand them; and first in a friendly Manner desire them to desist their unwarrantable Practices, and if that will not take Effect, then where are all our couragious young Men? Remember the saying of Solomon of old, that Oppression maketh a wise Man mad; stand together and forbid them Practicing in our Court, and rid the County of such Barbarity, and turn them out of the County. . . .

How Matters were carried on at the Court:

The Evening before the Court, there was a Liberty Pole set up, with a Union Flag at the Head of said Pole. Tuesday the 25th of July, it being the first Day of the Court, there was no less than two or three Hundred Liberty Boys, appeared under said Flag, in Defiance of the Gentlemen called L—yrs. The Court being called, the Court with the Grand-jury were admitted peaceably to enter the Court-House, but no L—yrs were admitted to go in; upon which the Court made Proposals to the Public, with Assurances, that they would redress the Grievances of the People, as far as lay in their Power; which in some Measure appeased the People, but who could not fully consent to make Way for the Lawyers to enter the Court-House. Wednesday the 26th Day of July in the Morning, it was again warmly insisted upon, by the Court Party, that the Liberty Pole should be taken down; a Gentlemen of said County asserted to the People, that the Lawyers had given up the Point, and would not seek for an Opportunity to enter the Court. Upon which in Obedience to the Court, the Pole was taken down, and all Matters appeared quiet; but when the Liberty Boys were in a Manner all dispersed, the Court was called. The Judges coming to the House, intermixed with the Lawyers, gave some few of the Liberty Boys Reason to suspect, that the Assertion from the aforesaid Gentlemen, was not fully observed; upon which they demanded the Reason of the Lawyers coming to enter the Court, but were answered with a general Attack from Judges, Sheriff, and Lawyers; who played away so furiously, that they soon overcame the small Number that opposed them, they being four to one, and so Judges, Sheriff, and Lawyers entered the Court. . . .

Bibliographic Note

General

Full annotation of the preceding essay and documents would require almost as much space as they occupy. Although the books and articles cited below represent only a small and unsystematic selection from the relevant literature, they should be enough to show a reader where to go for more detailed discussion of important subjects. Several themes of this volume will be elaborated by the author in a different study, *"Liberty and Property, Without Oppression": The Social Origins of Early American Law*, publication of which is anticipated in 1984, by the University of North Carolina Press for the Institute of Early American History and Culture at Williamsburg, Virginia.

For general analysis of the field, see Stanley N. Katz, "Looking Backward: The Early History of American Law," *University of Chicago Law Review*, 33 (1966), 867–884, along with Herbert A. Johnson, "American Colonial Legal History: A Historiographical Interpretation," in *Perspectives on Early American History: Essays in Honor of Richard B. Morris*, ed. Alden T. Vaughan and George A. Billias (New York, 1973), pp. 250–281. An excellent if somewhat dated survey is provided by David H. Flaherty, "An Introduction to Early American Legal History," in *Essays in the History of Early American Law*, ed. David H. Flaherty, (Chapel Hill, N.C., 1969), pp. 3–38. The other essays in this book make basic reading, as do those collected in George A. Billias (ed.), *Law and Authority in Colonial America* (Barre, Mass., 1965). Lawrence M. Friedman, *A History of American Law* (New York, 1973), pt. 1, is also helpful; and Richard M. Morris, *Studies in the History of American Law with Special Reference to the Seventeenth and Eighteenth Centuries* (New York, 1930), remains impressive in its breadth of coverage. For another kind of overview, see George Dargo, *Roots of the*

Republic: A New Perspective on Early American Constitutionalism (New York, 1974). There is a lengthy bibliography, extending to all the colonies, in Herbert A. Johnson, *Essays on New York Colonial Legal History* (Westport, Conn. 1981). The curious reader may also want to browse through issues of the *American Journal of Legal History*, consulting reviews as well as articles.

Good general surveys showing the English background of early American law include Alan Harding, *A Social History of English Law* (London, 1966), and J. H. Baker, *An Introduction to English Legal History*, 2nd ed. (London, 1979). Three collections of essays are also worth mentioning here: J. S. Cockburn (ed.), *Crime in England, 1550–1800* (London, 1977); John Brewer and John Styles (eds.), *An Ungovernable People: The English and Their Law in the Seventeenth and Eighteenth Centuries* (London, 1980); and Douglas Hay et al. (eds.), *Albion's Fatal Tree: Crime and Society in Eighteenth-Century England* (New York, 1975).

A Nation Among Peoples

It may be useful to begin Chapter 1 with the broad but informative treatment in Richard Hofstadter, *America at 1750: A Social Portrait* (New York, 1971), chaps. 1–4. Of many works bearing on Indian–white relations, a few articles will have to suffice: Wilcomb E. Washburn, "The Moral and Legal Justification for Dispossessing the Indians," in *Seventeenth-Century America: Essays in Colonial History*, ed. James M. Smith (Chapel Hill, N.C., 1959), pp. 15–32; Francis Jennings, "Virgin Land and Savage People," *American Quarterly*, 23 (1971), 519–541; George S. Snyderman, "Concepts of Land Ownership among the Iroquois and Their Neighbors," in *Symposium on Local Diversity in Iroquois Culture*, ed. William N. Fenton (Washington, D.C., 1951), pp. 13–34; and Anthony F. C. Wallace, "Political Organization and Land Tenure among the Northern Indians, 1600–1830," *Southwest Journal of Anthropology*, 13 (1957), 301–321. The classic study of white servitude is Abbot E. Smith, *Colonists in Bondage: White Servitude and Convict Labor in America, 1607–1776* (Durham, N.C., 1947). On the development of black chattel slavery, there is nothing to equal the concise sophistication of Winthrop D. Jordan, *White Over Black: American Attitudes Toward the Negro, 1550–1812* (Chapel Hill, N.C., 1968), pts. 1 and 2. See, too, William M. Wiecek, "The Statutory Law of Slavery and Race in the Thirteen Mainland Colonies of British America," *William and Mary Quarterly*, 3rd ser., 34 (1977), 258–280. The relationship of servitude to slavery is explored with subtlety in Edmund S. Morgan, *American Slavery, American Freedom: The Ordeal of Colonial Virginia* (New York, 1975). On Anglo–Dutch legal problems, see Herbert A. Johnson, "The Advent of Common Law in Colonial New York," in Billias, *Law and Authority*, pp. 74–91; Julius Goebel, Jr., "The Courts and the Law in Colonial New York, in Flaherty, *Essays*, pp. 245–277. Colonial naturalization law is examined in James H. Kettner, *The Development of American*

Citizenship: 1608–1870 (Chapel Hill, N.C., 1978), pt. 2; pt. 3 considers legal models of "conquest" and "discovery."

Religion and the State

See generally the valuable survey by David H. Flaherty, "Law and the Enforcement of Morals in Early America," *Perspectives in American History*, 5 (1971), 201–253. Although antiquated in its outlook, Philip A. Bruce, *Institutional History of Virginia in the Seventeenth Century* (New York, 1910), vol. 1, pt. 1, is filled with information concerning the ecclesiastical order. On religion in eighteenth-century Virginia, a good place to start is Robert E. Brown and B. Katherine Brown, *Virginia, 1705–1786: Democracy or Aristocracy?* (East Lansing, Mich., 1964), chap. 11. See, too, Rhys Isaac, *The Transformation of Virginia, 1740–1790* (Chapel Hill, N.C., 1982), pt. 2. The broad pattern of conflict between Anglicans and Nonconformists throughout the colonies is treated at length by Carl Bridenbaugh in *Mitre and Sceptre: Transatlantic Faiths, Ideas, Personalities, and Politics, 1689–1775* (New York, 1962). On the ambiguities of the Quaker experiment in Pennsylvania, see Frederick B. Tolles, *Meeting House and Counting House: The Quaker Merchants of Colonial Philadelphia, 1682–1763* (Chapel Hill, N.C., 1948). Studies of Puritanism are so numerous that the uninitiated reader will probably do best to begin with a historiographical essay, such as Michael McGiffert's "Puritan Studies in the 1960's," *William and Mary Quarterly*, 3rd ser., 27 (1970), 36–67. For an introduction to congregational discipline, see Emil Oberholzer, Jr., "The Church in New England Society," in Smith, *Seventeenth-Century America*, pp. 143–165. On Hebraic legislation, there is useful detail in Richard B. Morris, "Massachusetts and the Common Law: The Declaration of 1646," and Thorp L. Wolford, "The Laws and Liberties of 1648," both in Flaherty, *Essays*, pp. 135–185; and see generally George L. Haskins, *Law and Authority in Early Massachusetts: A Study in Tradition and Design* (New York, 1960). A conveniently short account of the legal issues raised by the witchcraft episode in Salem is available in Kenneth Ballard Murdock, *Increase Mather: The Foremost American Puritan* (Cambridge, Mass., 1925), chap. 17; for an intriguingly different perspective, see David Thomas Konig, *Law and Society in Puritan Massachusetts: Essex County, 1629–1692* (Chapel Hill, N.C., 1979), chaps. 6 and 7. Enforcement of moral legislation in eighteenth-century New England is discussed in William E. Nelson, *Americanization of the Common Law: The Impact of Legal Change on Massachusetts Society, 1760–1830* (Cambridge, Mass., 1975), chap. 3, and in Nelson, *Dispute and Conflict Resolution in Plymouth County, Massachusetts, 1725–1825* (Chapel Hill, N.C., 1981), chap. 2. These studies may be compared with Douglas Greenberg, *Crime and Law Enforcement in the Colony of New York, 1691–1776* (Ithaca, N.Y., 1976), and with Michael Stephen Hindus, *Prison and Plantation: Crime, Justice, and Authority in Massachusetts and South*

Carolina, 1767—1878 (Chapel Hill, N.C., 1980), chap. 3. Legal issues posed by the Great Awakening are better understood by looking at C. C. Goen, *Revivalism and Separatism in New England, 1740—1800* (New Haven, Conn., 1962), and Christopher M. Jedrey, *The World of John Cleaveland: Family and Community in Eighteenth-Century Massachusetts* (New York, 1979).

Community and Conflict

Many of the works already cited are obviously relevant for this chapter, along with those mentioned here. On early Puritan political theory, the most accessible discussion remains Edmund S. Morgan, *The Puritan Dilemma: The Story of John Winthrop* (Boston, 1958). An elegant comparative analysis is provided in G. B. Warden, "Law Reform in England and New England, 1620 to 1660," *William and Mary Quarterly*, 3rd ser., 35 (1978), 668—690. On the influence of English traditions, see Julius Goebel, Jr., "King's Law and Local Custom in Seventeenth Century New England," in Flaherty, *Essays*, pp. 83—120. Conditions in the seventeenth-century Chesapeake region are described in Bruce, *Institutional History*, vol.1, pt. 3; see also, for example, Raphael Semmes, *Crime and Punishment in Early Maryland* (Baltimore, 1938), and Joseph H. Smith, "The Foundations of Law in Maryland: 1634—1715," in Billias, *Law and Authority*, pp. 92—115. Stabilizing tendencies in Maryland toward the end of the seventeenth century are emphasized by Lois Green Carr and David William Jordan, *Maryland's Revolution of Government, 1689—1692* (Ithaca, N.Y., 1974). Fencing law is considered in Morris, *Studies*, chap. 4. Konig, *Law and Society*, chap. 2, is especially illuminating on land policies in early New England; it should be supplemented by Philip J. Greven, Jr., *Four Generations: Population, Land, and Family in Colonial Andover, Massachusetts* (Ithaca, N.Y., 1970). On the structure of the New England family, the latter work is also outstanding, as is John Demos, *A Little Commonwealth: Family Life in Plymouth Colony* (New York, 1970). Morris, *Studies*, chap. 3, is still a valuable discussion of women's rights throughout the colonies. Further readings on this subject might include Roger Thompson, *Women in Stuart England and America: A Comparative Study* (London, 1974), chap. 8; Nancy F. Cott, "Divorce and the Changing Status of Women in Eighteenth-Century Massachusetts," *William and Mary Quarterly*, 3rd ser., 33 (1976), 586—614; Linda K. Kerber, *Women of the Republic: Intellect and Ideology in Revolutionary America* (Chapel Hill, N.C., 1980), chap. 6; Joan R. Gunderson and Gwen Victor Gampel, "Married Women's Legal Status in Eighteenth-Century New York and Virginia," *William and Mary Quarterly*, 3rd ser., 39 (1982), 114—134. The peculiarities of New England's inheritance law are explained in George L. Haskins, "The Beginnings of Partible Inheritance in the American Colonies," and Charles McLean Andrews, "The Influence of Colonial Conditions as Illustrated in the Connecticut Intestacy Law," both in Flaherty, *Essays*, pp. 204—244, 336—366; changing circumstances are emphasized, for example, in John J. Waters, "Family, Inheritance, and Migration in Colonial New

England: The Evidence from Guilford, Connecticut," *William and Mary Quarterly*, 3rd ser., 39 (1982), 64–86. For comparative purposes, see Lorena S. Walsh, " 'Till Death Us Do Part: Marriage and Family in Seventeenth-Century Maryland," in *The Chesapeake in the Seventeenth Century: Essays on Anglo-American Society*, ed. Thad W. Tate and David L. Ammerman (Chapel Hill, N.C., 1979), pp. 126–152; Lois Green Carr, "The Development of the Maryland Orphans' Court, 1654–1715," in *Law, Society, and Politics in Early Maryland*, ed. Aubrey C. Land et al. (Baltimore, 1977), pp. 41–62; Brown and Brown, *Virginia*, chap. 4; C. Ray Keim, "Primogeniture and Entail in Colonial Virginia," *William and Mary Quarterly*, 3rd ser., 25 (1968), 545–586; and Daniel Blake Smith, *Inside the Great House: Planter Family Life in Eighteenth-Century Chesapeake Society* (Ithaca, N.Y., 1980), chap. 6. Issac, *Transformation of Virginia*, pt. 1, describes the Chesapeake gentry culture that emerged in the eighteenth century. A full account of the 1741 "plot" in New York is available in *The New York Conspiracy*, ed. Thomas J. Davis (Boston, 1971). On community in eighteenth-century New England, compare Nelson, *Americanization of the Common Law*, chap. 4, or Nelson, *Dispute and Conflict Resolution*, chap. 3, with Greven, *Four Generations*, or Robert A. Gross, *The Minutemen and Their World* (New York, 1976). See, too, David Grayson Allen, *In English Ways: The Movement of Societies and the Transferral of English Local Law and Custom to Massachusetts Bay in the Seventeenth Century* (Chapel Hill, N.C., 1981), chap. 7; Douglas Lamar Jones, "The Strolling Poor: Transiency in Eighteenth-Century Massachusetts," *Journal of Social History*, 8 (Spring 1975), 28–54; and Richard L. Bushman, "Massachusetts Farmers and the Revolution," in *Society, Freedom, and Conscience: The American Revolution in Virginia, Massachusetts, and New York*, ed. Richard M. Jellison (New York, 1976), pp. 77–124. The situation along the Hudson River is treated thoroughly by Sung Bok Kim, *Landlord and Tenant in Colonial New York: Manorial Society, 1664–1775* (Chapel Hill, N.C., 1978). On the legitimacy of the colonial "mob," see Pauline Maier, *From Resistance to Revolution: Colonial Radicals and the Development of American Opposition to Britain, 1765–1776* (New York, 1972), chap. 1.

The Stresses of Empire

For Chapter 4, which concludes with the Revolution, the basic literature is vast and relatively familiar. Bernard Bailyn, *The Origins of American Politics* (New York, 1968), offers the best analytic overview of the Anglo-American political system. Bushman, "Massachusetts Farmers," relates the Andros episode to later concerns of New Englanders; other prerevolutionary issues are well summarized in Maier, *From Resistance to Revolution*, chap. 1. On English policies toward the colonial judiciary, see Joseph H. Smith, "Administrative Control of the Courts of the American Plantations," in Flaherty, *Essays*, pp. 281–335, and Joseph H. Smith, *Appeals to the Privy Council from the American Plantations* (New York, 1950). *Winthrop v.*

Lechmere is the specific subject of Andrews, "Influence of Colonial Conditions." For other issues of judicial politics, see Carl W. Ubbelohde, *The Vice-Admiralty Courts and the American Revolution* (Chapel Hill, N.C., 1960), and Stanley N. Katz, "The Politics of Law in Colonial America: Controversies over Chancery Courts and Equity Law in the Eighteenth Century," *Perspectives in American History*, 5 (1971), 257–284. The new formalism in legal practice is discussed generally by Stephen Botein, "The Legal Profession in Colonial North America," in *Lawyers in Early Modern Europe and America*, ed. Wilfred Prest, (London, 1981), pp. 129–146. More specifically, see John M. Murrin, "The Legal Transformation: The Bench and Bar of Eighteenth-Century Massachusetts," in *Colonial America: Essays in Politics and Social Development*, ed. Stanley N. Katz (Boston, 1971), pp. 415–449; Milton M. Klein, "The Rise of the New York Bar: The Legal Career of William Livingston," in Flaherty, *Essays*, pp. 392–417; and A. G. Roeber, *Faithful Magistrates and Republican Lawyers: Creators of Virginia Legal Culture, 1680–1810* (Chapel Hill, N.C., 1981). Particulars of the Zenger case are available in *A Brief Narrative of the Case and Trial of John Peter Zenger*, ed. Stanley N. Katz (Cambridge, Mass., 1963). The authoritative study of revolutionary constitutionalism is Bernard Bailyn, *The Ideological Origins of the American Revolution* (Cambridge, Mass., 1967). On the role of lawyers in the Revolution, see Erwin C. Surrency, "The Lawyer and the Revolution," *American Journal of Legal History*, 8 (1964), 125–135; Milton M. Klein, "New York Lawyers and the Coming of the American Revolution," *New York History*, 55 (1974), 383–407. On popular antagonism toward the profession, see Patricia U. Bonomi, *A Factious People: Politics and Society in Colonial New York* (New York, 1971), chap. 7; James P. Whittenburg, "Planters, Merchants, and Lawyers: Social Change and the Origins of the North Carolina Regulation," *William and Mary Quarterly*, 3rd ser., 34 (1977), 215–238; and Larry R. Gerlach, *Prologue to Independence: New Jersey in the Coming of the American Revolution* (New Brunswick, N.J., 1976), chap. 6. Kettner, *Development of American Citizenship*, pt. 3, outlines the Patriot case for independence; its relation to religious separatism is discussed by Stephen Botein, "Religion and Politics in Revolutionary New England: Natural Rights Reconsidered," in *Party and Political Opposition in Revolutionary America*, ed. Patricia U. Bonomi (Tarrytown, N.Y., 1980), pp. 13–34. The importance of Massachusetts in the legal history of the Revolution is stressed particularly by John Phillip Reid, *In a Defiant Stance: The Conditions of Law in Massachusetts Bay, the Irish Comparison, and the Coming of the American Revolution* (University Park, Pa., 1977). On the conservatism of the revolutionary bench in Massachusetts, see John D. Cushing, "The Judiciary and Public Opinion in Revolutionary Massachusetts," in Billias, *Law and Authority*, pp. 168–186.

Finally, a brief word of advice concerning language may be helpful. Although every effort has been made to avoid obscure terminology, there is no getting away from the difficulties of seventeenth- and eighteenth-century prose. One or another reference book in law might be recommended, but none matches the *Oxford English Dictionary* as a source of historical insight.

Index

Adams, John: as legal reformer, 60; opposed to Hutchinson family, 63–64; as revolutionary ideologue, 66–67
Adams, Sam, revolutionary leader, 119
Admiralty, as agency of imperial administration, 51
"Agreements of the People," as formulated by radical English Puritans, 33
Alexander VI, pope, 5
American Revolution, legal aspects of, 3–4, 64–67, 119, 123
Andrews, Charles McLean, historian, 3
Andros, Edmund, governor of Dominion of New England, 51–52, 54, 66
Anglicans. *See* Church of England
Art of Pleading. See Livingston, William
Attorneys. *See* Legal profession
Avery, Benjamin, English dissenting leader, 28

Bacon, Nathaniel, Virginia councilor, 11
Bacon's Rebellion, 11
Baptists: in Virginia, 22; in New England, 28
Barbados, professional lawyers in, 63
Barristers. *See* Legal profession
Belcher, Jonathan, as colonial agent, 112
Berkeley, William, governor of Virginia, 11
Bishop of London, in imperial administrative system, 51
Blackstone, William, on Christianity, 30
Blair, James, Anglican official in Virginia, 20
Board of Trade, as agency of imperial administration, 50–51, 54
"Body of Liberties." *See* "Laws and Liberties"

Cabot, John, as "discoverer," 5–6
Cambridge Platform of Church Discipline, adoption, 24
Canassateego, Iroquois negotiator, 70
Chancery. *See* Equity jurisdiction

135

About the Author

STEPHEN BOTEIN is associate professor of history at Michigan State University. Since receiving his Ph.D. from Harvard University, he has published articles on early American printers, clergymen, and lawyers, and has spent a year as a fellow of the Davis Center for Historical Research at Princeton University. Currently he is working on a book about "expertise" in eighteenth-century America.

A Note on the Type

The text of this book was set in a computer version of Times Roman, designed by Stanley Morison for *The Times* (London) and first introduced by that newspaper in 1932.

Among typographers and designers of the twentieth century, Stanley Morison has been a strong forming influence as typographical adviser to the English Monotype Corporation, as a director of two distinguished English publishing houses, and as a writer of sensibility, erudition, and keen practical sense.

Typography by Barbara Sturman. Cover design by Maria Epes. Composition by The Saybrook Press, Inc., Old Saybrook, Connecticut. Printed and bound by Banta Company, Menasha, Wisconsin.

BORZOI BOOKS
IN LAW AND AMERICAN SOCIETY

Law and American History

EARLY AMERICAN LAW AND SOCIETY
Stephen Botein, *Michigan State University*

This volume consists of an essay dealing with the nature of law and early American socioeconomic development from the first settlements to 1776. The author shows how many legal traditions sprang both from English experience and from the influence of the New World. He explores the development of transatlantic legal structures in order to show how they helped rationalize intercolonial affairs. Mr. Botein also emphasizes the relationship between law and religion. The volume includes a pertinent group of documents for classroom discussion, and a bibliographic essay.

LAW IN THE NEW REPUBLIC: *Private Law and the Public Estate*
George Dargo, *Brookline, Massachusetts*

Though the American Revolution had an immediate and abiding impact on American public law (e.g., the formation of the federal and state constitutions), its effect on private law (e.g., the law of contracts, tort law) was less direct but of equal importance. Through essay and documents, Mr. Dargo examines post-Revolutionary public and private reform impulses and finds a shifting emphasis from public to private law which he terms "privatization." To further illustrate the tension between public and private law, the author develops a case study (the Batture land controversy in New Orleans) in early nineteenth century legal, economic, and political history. The volume includes a wide selection of documents and a bibliographic essay.

LAW IN ANTEBELLUM SOCIETY: *Legal Change and Economic Expansion*
Jamil Zainaldin, *Washington, D.C.*

This book examines legal change and economic expansion in the first half of the nineteenth century, integrating major themes in the development of law with key historical themes. Through a series of topical essays and the use of primary source materials, it describes how political, social, and economic interests and values influence law making. The book's focus is on legislation and the common law.

LAW AND THE NATION, 1865–1912
Jonathan Lurie, *Rutgers University*

Using the Fourteenth Amendment as the starting point for his essay, Mr. Lurie examines the ramifications of this landmark constitutional provision on the economic and social development of America in the years following the Civil War. He also explores important late nineteenth-century developments in legal education, and concludes his narrative with some insights on law and social change in the first decade of the twentieth century. The volume is highlighted by a documents section containing statutes, judicial opinions, and legal briefs, with appropriate questions for classroom discussion. Mr. Lurie's bibliographic essay provides information to stimulate further investigation of this period.

ORDERED LIBERTY: *Legal Reform in the Twentieth Century*
Gerald L. Fetner, *University of Chicago*

In an interpretive essay, the author examines the relationship between several major twentieth-century reform movements (e.g., Progressivism, New Deal, and the Great Society) and the law. He shows how policy makers turned increasingly to the legal community for assistance in accommodating economic and social conflict, and how the legal profession responded by formulating statutes, administrative agencies, and private arrangements. Mr. Fetner also discusses how the organization and character of the legal profession were affected by these social changes. Excerpts from relevant documents illustrate issues discussed in the essay. A bibliographic essay is included.

Law and Philosophy

DISCRIMINATION AND REVERSE DISCRIMINATION
R. Kent Greenawalt, *Columbia Law School*

Using discrimination and reverse discrimination as a model, Mr. Greenawalt examines the relationship between law and ethics. He finds that the proper role of law cannot be limited to grand theory concerning individual liberty and social restraint, but must address what law can effectively discover and accomplish. Such concepts as distributive and compensatory justice and utility are examined in the context of preferential treatment for blacks and other minorities. The analysis draws heavily on the Supreme Court's Bakke decision. The essay is followed by related documents, primarily judicial opinions, with notes and questions, and a bibliography.

THE LEGAL ENFORCEMENT OF MORALITY
Thomas Grey, *Stanford Law School*

This book deals with the traditional issue of whether morality can be legislated and enforced. It consists of an introductory essay and legal texts on three issues: the enforcement of sexual morality, the treatment of human remains, and the duties of potential rescuers. The author shows how philosophical problems differ from classroom hypotheticals when they are confronted in a legal setting. He illustrates this point using material from statutes, regulations, judicial opinions, and law review commentaries. Mr. Grey reviews the celebrated Hart-Devlin debate over the legitimacy of prohibiting homosexual acts. He places the challenging problem of how to treat dead bodies, arising out of developments in the technology of organ transplantation, in the context of the debate over morals enforcement, and discusses the Good Samaritan as an issue concerning the propriety of the legal enforcement of moral duties.

LEGAL REASONING
Martin Golding, *Duke University*

This volume is a blend of text and readings. The author explores the many sides to legal reasoning—as a study in judicial psychology and, in a more narrow sense, as an inquiry into the "logic" of judicial decision making. He shows how judges justify their rulings, and gives examples of the kinds of arguments they use. He challenges the notion that judicial reasoning is rationalization; instead, he argues that judges are guided by a deep concern for consistency and by a strong need to have their decisions stand as a measure for the future conduct of individuals. *(Forthcoming in 1984)*

Law and American Literature

LAW AND AMERICAN LITERATURE
A one-volume collection of the following three essays:

Law as Form and Theme in American Letters
Carl S. Smith, *Northwestern University*

The author explores the interrelationships between law aned literature generally and between American law and American literature in particular. He explores first the literary qualities of legal writing and then the attitudes of major American writers toward the law. Throughout, he studies the links between the legal and literary imaginations. He finds that legal writing has many literary qualities that are essential to its function, and he points out that American writers have long been wary of the power of the law and its special language, speaking out as a compensating voice for the ideal of justice.

Innocent Criminal or Criminal Innocence: The Trial in American Fiction
John McWilliams, *Middlebury College*

Mr. McWilliams explores how law functions as a standard for conduct in a number of major works of American literature, including Cooper's *The Pioneers,* Melville's *Billy Budd,* Dreiser's *An American Tragedy,* and Wright's *Native Son.* Each of these books ends in a criminal trial, in which the reader is asked to choose between his emotional sympathy for the victim and his rational understanding of society's need for criminal sanctions. The author compares these books with James Gould Cozzens' *The Just and the Unjust,* a study of a small town legal system, in which the people's sense of justice contravenes traditional authority.

Law and Lawyers in American Popular Culture
Maxwell Bloomfield, *Catholic University of America*

Melding law, literature, and the American historical experience into a single essay, Mr. Bloomfield discusses popular images of the lawyer. The author shows how contemporary values and attitudes toward the law are reflected in fiction. He concentrates on two historical periods: antebellum America and the Progressive era. He examines fictional works which were not always literary classics, but which exposed particular legal mores. An example of such a book is Winston Churchill's *A Far Country* (1915), a story of a successful corporation lawyer who abandons his practice to dedicate his life to what he believes are more socially desirable objectives.